The Presents of Eagles: Lessons in Life, Love,
Mentoring and Other Meaningful Relationships
Written By Lora Reed
With
Photographs by Dana Reed

With gratitude to the eagles and eaglets, feathered or not,
who model how to soar to our potential.
And especially to Bevvie, Donna, Tammy, Karen, Amy,
Maria & Pastor Mark
for their encouragement and great insight!

# Preface

One of the most beautiful New Testament Bible scriptures instructs us to, "Look at the birds of the air; they do not sow or reap or store away in barns, and yet our heavenly Father feeds them. Are you not much more valuable than they?" (Matthew 6: 26 NIV). Another scripture charges, "…ask the animals, and they will teach you; or the birds in the sky, and they will tell you; or speak to the earth, and it will teach you; or let the fish in the sea inform you. Which of all these does not know that the hand of the Lord has done this?" (**Job 12:7-9**, NIV). And, in Isaiah, we are told that, "…those who hope in the Lord will renew their strength. They will soar on wings like eagles; they will run and not grow weary, and they will walk and not be faint." (40: 31, NIV). How often do busy contemporary humans take such scriptures literally? How often do we take the time to watch?

This book is an attempt to consider lessons learned from watching a family of eagles in the context of a Florida Nature preserve during the first decade of the 21st century. Clearly, it is not the first book to ponder such lessons; nor will it be the last. However, the book shares a unique perspective. It is a fictionalized account of how people's lives were touched, transformed in some cases, by a family of eagles who graciously reminded them of many important life lessons. The stories are true, but dates, names and personal information about the people and the Preserve have been changed to protect individual privacy.

Thankfully, the people watching the eagles were willing to consider the birds of the air. Thankfully, a magnificent young family of American Bald Eagles was willing to share their teaching and learning experiences with humans. As people of the Preserve who watched these extraordinary birds we were taught lessons on life, love, mentoring and meaningful relationships. This book shares those lessons with you. We hope you will enjoy the <u>Presents of Eagles</u> as much as we have enjoyed learning and sharing them – so far.

## Table of Contents

# Chapter 1 Welcome to the Preserve

The view looking northwest from Humphrey's Preserve

In 2007, Florida real estate sales were booming at unprecedented rates. Several estimates suggested that thousands of people per week were moving to the state and it seemed, for the most part, most of them wanted to buy homes. For some folks, such as real estate agents, mortgage bankers, building contractors, construction workers, plumbers, painters, electricians, and employees of community building departments, this was a time of tremendous prosperity. Many home values doubled and tripled seemingly overnight. But for other people, such as those who could not afford to move from where they already lived in Florida, it meant access to beachfronts and the beauty of the natural phenomena was increasingly endangered and often severely constricted. Ironically, the same natural beauty that attracted so many new Florida residents was, to more enduring Floridians, threatened by the building boom. This was the dilemma for human and non-human Florida residents alike. If people weren't careful, it was going to be the case for future generations as well (see Florida Aquatic Preserves 2012).

As one Florida family that had lived in a coastal community for many years observed the real estate mayhem, they considered the disposition of a large piece of land that had been owned by their family for years. The Humphrey's observed other parcels of property adjacent to their hundreds of acres being bought and cleared for upscale single family homes, and they saw locals increasingly at risk of losing the delicate ecology of a formerly agrarian waterside community. Too many new projects would diminish the limited wildlife habitat. Too many new homes meant less accessible coast for the people who could not afford to build in these neighborhoods. Sadly, new homeowners also sometimes inadvertently encroached upon the wildlife habitat that was there long before the boom; it was something the new home owners enjoyed but seldom understood. Consequently, some more silent endangered locals (such as herons, ospreys, pelicans, mullet, hermit crabs and coyotes) were at risk of being displaced. And, these residents' ancestors had been in the area for multiple generations; these creatures were not only home, they knew no better place to go.

Too often, the non-human costs of the Florida real estate boom could not be accurately calculated in any one transaction. Luckily, many Floridians recognize that much of Florida's natural beauty lies along its coastlines. And, in this case, even more fortunately, among Florida's conservation and civic-minded families was the Humphrey's. They announced their intent to make available for sale to the county government almost 500 acres of prime waterfront property comprised of marshlands, open waterways, and potential nature trails. It was offered at an affordable price and as a potential legacy for the community to enjoy long after the boom was over.

The Humphrey's property was a haven for native plants and animals, including birds, fish, and endangered species such as gopher tortoises which are known as a keystone species because their digging contributes to proliferation of about 350 other species (Florida Fish and Wildlife Conservation Commission). The property had, at one time, been used commercially to grow palm trees and then later, mums. After interest in its agricultural use declined, the land had become fallow, spoiled by human discards such as abandoned pleasure crafts and fishing boats alike. Essentially, in recent years, the beautiful piece of wetlands had become an illegal dump.

Now, at a critical time in Florida history, the land that was to become Humphrey's Preserve was offered up for restoration. Its value had been reassessed, but not just as a short term real estate investment. The Humphrey's wanted current and future generations to know that key community leaders shared their realizable and beautiful dream of preserving the natural integrity of the beautiful waterside hamlet.

So, with waterfront properties booming all around them, the Humphrey's and others realized the acreage was more valuable to many as a Preserve than as any one single home. They began to assist in ensuring its protection as precious and protected Florida wetlands. As a result, they began to enjoy a stewardship role in keeping the land public for encouraging fisheries, exotic bird rookeries and other endangered Florida treasures that were indigenous to the tropical habitat along the Gulf of Mexico.

The Humphrey's and other locals, including government officials, scholars, key citizens and volunteers worked out details of a purchase that would have been difficult for any stakeholder to resist, and the community acquired the property as a preserve. They named it, most appropriately, Humphrey's Preserve. It is now one of many such parcels in the county – destined to preserve Nature and the character of a beautiful coastal community. And, as you will learn in this story, Humphrey's Preserve is part of an even grander design. It is a small, critical element of a much, much bigger picture.

# Chapter 2 – Part of a Bigger Picture

Ducks and a bicyclist sharing the thoroughfare near the
Preserve

It soon became obvious to the people who visited that Humphrey's Preserve was an Eden, almost pristine acreage that was well-looked-after as a habitat, and that had recently escaped imminent danger in the real estate boom. Its restoration involved the cooperation of an array of grant writers, as well as the assistance of federal, state, and community agencies in concert – each with the end goal of restoring the coastal property to its natural state so that it would serve people, environment and researchers alike. Its maintenance was accomplished, in large part, to a corps of local volunteers. Its development would be ongoing, a collaboration of scientists and policymakers from many agencies, assisted by students from multiple disciplines and a variety of public and private academic institutions. Humphrey's Preserve was clearly a gift that the community continued to appreciate and, because of their gratitude, the gift continued to contribute many other evolving gifts.

Many exotic invasive species were removed from the Preserve by teams consisting of experts and volunteers. Canals and waterways were reconfigured and recut by groups including, but not limited to, the Army Corps of Engineers. Tidal water flow was considered, reconsidered and redirected to encourage fish hatcheries and fish redistribution. It was also analyzed for other benefits, such as regular re-nourishment of brackish waters wherein delicacies that entice water birds, dolphins, manatees, raptors and other Florida wildlife would thrive both initially and in the future. And thrive the animals did. With each small effort, the Preserve became even more beautiful.

In 2008, when Humphrey's Preserve officially opened, mullet could be seen jumping in the waterways. Ospreys could be heard, as if they were laughing in the skies. Roseate spoonbills created iridescent silhouettes on the horizon. And visitors often stopped in awe. The splendid beauty of Nature, as part of the community, made local and tourist take notice – and consider that they were part of something bigger, something that increased their knowledge and appreciation of Nature as they got healthier by exercising in the wonderful place.

Oddly, when the real estate bubble finally burst, the Preserve became even more valuable as a free-admission-to-the-public resource that gave sanctuary, joy and pleasure to all who visited. Both locals and tourists, of all ages, genders, ethnicities and walks of life, began to bike, roller blade, kayak, fish, and photograph in the area. Each guest's visit was a meditation, a ritual of whatever form the weary traveler needed. Whether they came to work or play, each visitor left the Preserve knowing it was the perfect environment for humans and animals to thrive in interdependence and appreciation of each other. It was a revitalized Eden, an experimental and experiential lesson in sustainability, stewardship and community. It was becoming an incubator for rejuvenation of human energy and spirit, as well as the property and the wildlife that were all part of the same equation.

Perhaps even more astounding was that the Preserve's founders seemed to have foreseen that collaboration among stakeholders such as the conservationists, teachers and students, youth groups, naturalists, engineers, townspeople, researchers, school clubs, environmental interns, retirees and other volunteers was essential to the health of the land and to all members of the community. Like siblings of an extended family at Thanksgiving, each stakeholder brought a unique offering, his or her best 'dish' or talent to celebrate and serve in the restoration of 'home' where plants and wildlife once again began to flourish. In a place where most other properties had been exhausted by the influx of development that fulfilled dreams for individual families, the Preserve was rapidly becoming repopulated with native species and appreciative inhabitants. It was abuzz with vibrant energy.

In the mixed blessing that had precluded the recent Florida real estate bust, development obstacles that had inhibited access to the bay for the majority of locals rapidly vanished – along with many people's dreams. But acquisition of the Preserve salvaged an inkling of rare connection to the Earth as 'home'. Strangely, the death of the boom and the birth of the Preserve made locals realize they were indeed stewards of this marvelous treasure, this gem on Florida's Gulf Coast. In 2008 when Humphrey's Preserve opened to the public, everyone knew that, like the rest of Nature, it would never be 'finished'; it would remain an evolving work in progress. And as word got out, the Preserve became a sanctuary for visitors. It has also continued to become an even more remarkable vehicle for unlikely collaborations of partners in restoration. People have continued to think of ways their stewardship can benefit human and non-human residents and visitors for generations to come. Humphrey's Preserve still affords freedom and beauty for walkers, bikers, anglers and other naturalists. More amazing, it is a place to experience the largesse of birds and other creatures that seem to have expressed their gratitude by letting humans observe and learn from their presence, from a safe distance for both.

These are stories of some of the many gifts shared with humans at the preserve; specifically, these are tales of an eagle family who graced the locals and other visitors with their presents. We begin at the beginning, when...

# Chapter 3 – The Eagles Have Landed

One of the adult eagles surveying the Preserve from the highest perch available

In early September 2009, a pair of young eagles decided to make their home in Humphrey's Preserve. No doubt, they, like their human counterparts, realized what an amazing place it was to exercise, fish, and spend lovely days developing their young family. As is typical of Southern American Bald Eagles, the male arrived first. Then, about a week later (just before Labor Day), his lovely spouse appeared. Together they scouted the area for places where they might build a nest that they might use as 'home' for the eaglets they would hatch in the winter. Like so many humans who had visited the preserve, the young couple was eager to explore ways to make this a place where they and their offspring would be able to enjoy the bounty of Nature.

Soon after the young eagles' arrival, it became evident to some of the locals that the eagles had decided the Preserve was a brilliant place to raise their family. The pair selected a stately Australian pine in which to build a nest. And, on regular occasions, the few locals that recognized what they were doing were exhilarated by observing the two flying; carrying twigs, fresh greens and other items suitable for use in construction of a nest. As if that was not sensational enough, a few onlookers knew that eagles do not live in nests most of the time, so word began to spread that soon the Preserve might be home to eaglets. Typically, eagles construct and return to nests only prior to mating season. Then, during the late fall and winter, their nests serve as shelters for purposes of egg incubation and child rearing, teaching their eaglet progenies the many things they must learn in order to survive.

The Australian pine tree the young eagle couple had selected in autumn of 2009 appeared to be durable. It looked resilient enough to sustain a nest-house that would hold both Mom and Dad and any eaglets they might breed in late fall of that year, as well as in future years to come. You see, although eagles often migrate for the summer months, when possible, they return to the same nest year after year for their mating season. And, when possible, eagles mate for life.

At first in September of 2009, only a few of the local people noticed the eagles. After all, most people came to the Preserve for other reasons, such as their own exercise and other activities that demanded a form of healthy meditation or what might be described as self-interest properly understood. And, in all fairness, the rigorousness of the people's activities often distracted them from observing birds and other wildlife. Besides, so much beauty abounded in the Preserve at any given moment that, perhaps luckily for them, the eagles often blended into the stunning ecology. But the few folks who did pay attention quickly realized that the young eagles had two offspring that fall; and, in April, as is typical of eagles in the southern United States, all four of the birds migrated to places unknown, as did many of the people.

Migration of birds and people is quite common in Florida. So, in early fall of 2010, the birds were slightly ahead of most people who returned to the Preserve. Once again, the male returned first and he began sprucing up the nest. About a week later his spouse, along with their two children, arrived at the Preserve. Eagles often travel as extended family. Undoubtedly they realize that, most often, there is safety in numbers and young eagles typically take from three to five years to mature. During that time it is common for juvenile birds to stay near their parents. Adolescent eagles, like many of their human counterparts, will even try to return home after they have moved out. In the case of the eagles, that means they sometimes frequent the nest they were raised in during winter (mating and incubation seasons). Although the young eagles' parents may appear to be lenient, when a new egg arrives, the adolescents are told – in no uncertain terms – it is time for them to move out.

In autumn of 2010, when the eagle couple and their youngsters returned, by most local eagle-loving-humans' accounts, the pair was now about eight years old. By the time the whole family arrived, more locals had become eager to watch them. Some people undoubtedly thought the birds' arrival signaled the approach of autumn, the beginning of the end of hurricane season. Most people knew it was the onset of the birds' annual mating ritual. In each case, to the observers, the return of the eagles was cause for celebration!

One local was a house Painter and a regular volunteer at the Preserve. He spent weekend mornings with a scope set up, patiently, kindly and generously sharing views of the birds, along with eagle stories. Any passerby who was interested enough was welcome to stop and talk. Another local, a former home Builder, rode his bike to the Preserve each day. This was a form of exercise and meditation. It was also his way of working off frustration. You see, by this time the recession has begun to hit hard; there were few houses being built, and few houses being painted. The Builder and Painter learned they had much in common, and they began to become good friends as they observed the eagles soar.

The Builder and the Painter both eagerly took on roles as stewards, along with the Rangers and other volunteers who cared deeply for the historic and beautiful Preserve that housed many wonders, stories, and healthy people and critter activities. The Rangers, the Builder and the Painter led others who entered the Preserve by serving them in the spirit of community. But most of all, the Painter and the Builder began to take great care to watch for birds – especially the eagles, who were also watching them and giving them a new form of strength. The humans and the birds seemed engaged in a reciprocal process of assisting each other.

As time went by that fall, more local and visiting humans began to look forward to seeing the eagles, and learning about their annual migration. The people ascertained that the eagle pair had migrated to the Preserve since they had become mature enough to start a family. They would likely return as a strong and cooperative team that would stay together until one or both of them died. The adolescents who followed them back were learning from the adults' mentoring. And just as the Preserve had become the pair's home, it was likely to be home to the adolescents until one or both of them took a mate and moved on to create their own space either here or in another appropriate environment.

Most other American Bald Eagles who had scouted out the area had elected to move inland to enjoy taller pines and less populated areas. In Florida, the bounty of fish and other food sources that live in and near lakes and rivers is impressive. The other eagles that had moved inland were further away from humans, but the pair of Preserve eagles was destined to become local legends. And as the economy got tougher, their return signified, on some sacred level, that both the people and birds had made it through one more year of a tough time. Somehow birds and the people seemed tied together; and on some level, no matter how difficult things might become, the birds and the people were destined to survive and thrive. They each had hope and seemed to know they were supposed to look out for one another. If they did, they would somehow thrive interdependently as long as they did their best to 'soar' together.

The eagles' return also signified that, although life might get difficult, it was still okay. As long as humanity and the rest of Nature worked together, there was hope for the next generation for both. Some of the humans began to learn eagle-facts, such as that although American bald eagles were taken off the Federal List of Endangered and Threatened Wildlife in 2007, and their numbers are increasing, they were and are still protected by the Migratory Bird Treaty Act and the Bald and Golden Eagle Protection Act. Their demise usually results from careless or deliberate human interaction in the form of poisoning, gunshot wounds, electrocution or car collision. In the wild, an eagle's death usually results from natural causes at around age 30-35, or in earlier years by hypothermia and/or starvation.

In the fall of 2010, the return of the Humphrey's Pair signaled survival and bounty for everyone for another season. The feathered symbols of freedom, power, loyalty and independence demonstrated it was still possible to soar. And their human following continued to grow, as did the numbers of visitors to the Preserve. The eagles had created an unlikely shadowing that watched and adored them from afar. This was especially paradoxical since humanity had long been the greatest threat to this majestic species.

# Chapter 4 – Meet Some of the Human Family

The Builder winding through the Preserve on one of many bike paths

When the Preserve opened in 2008, a few of the locals were immediately interested in exploring its significance for them and the community. Among them was a young man who lived nearby. He was employed in an occupation that was lucrative and expanding, but he was immediately captivated by the potential for his relationship to the Preserve. He began visiting regularly, riding his bike, walking the trails with his wife and children, and envisioning how grand it would be to spend his time developing a dream that was rapidly evolving in partnership with Nature and community. As the Preserve required more complex coordination and stewardship, a position was created for a primary Ranger. The young man applied, and as naturally as he could claim his right livelihood, he was awarded the honor of the position of Ranger. He was perfect for the job. For all intents and purposes, he became the Preserve's chief steward. Although other governmental employees may have held more sway, and an array of volunteers from various organizations and walks of life regularly served other objectives focused on caring for and developing the preserve, few were as naturally at home there as the Ranger. He seemed to blend in among the creatures and plants that somehow knew that he meant them no harm. Daily, other visitors would see the Ranger tending pathways, pulling out invasive pepper plants and performing physically demanding tasks that most would find difficult. But he did so with a smile and a kind word for each passerby, as though each person was a welcome recipient of community hospitality and as though maintenance of the Preserve was his highest calling. The Ranger was honored to care for the place that so many were coming to love. His responses to tasks and to questions from passersby were based on the instincts of a person performing work inherent to his own nature, as well as to the needs of the community at large.

From the time the Preserve was opened to the public, its regular visitors also included the Builder, the Painter and the Teacher. The Builder was a craftsperson whose work-life had halted immediately with the burst of the real estate bubble. On the bright side, he and his business partner, a friend since high school, were not among the folks who lost millions due to speculative over-building during the boom. On the not so bright side, they had never had millions, were both cautious investors and had over time endured many losses together. This one meant their livelihoods dissipated in a "poof!" that was the middle of a lifelong dream of building neighborhoods and beautiful homes for families. Their opportunity to engage in constructive work they loved as long as they wanted had ended. For the Builder, it also meant the line of work he had been engaged in all of his life was no longer available to him. He would have to learn new ways to help support his family and others who needed assistance in order to have a better foundation for life.

The Builder was in his early sixties when the recession hit. At first, his reaction was to grieve and be heartbroken about plans he had made for his final working years. He knew this meant he was close to the end of creating meaningful, quality work opportunities for other craftspeople too. As he considered the ramifications of the recession, Humphrey's Preserve became more than a place for him to ride his bicycle. It became the sanctuary where he could re-evaluate life and appreciate the beauty of Nature where he had grown up. It was a respite, a place to be grateful for the ability to marvel at the simple beauty he had been afforded for many of his days. As a result, the Preserve became a sacred venue for photographing creatures and plants that, like him, had endured in this striking habitat despite hazards of the troubling times. Indeed, the Preserve became an environment wherein he and his situation were forced to be examined from multiple perspectives. It was where he began to consider other things he wanted to do with his life.

By early September 2010 when the eagles returned to the area, the Builder had not only resigned himself to his new situation, he was making the best of it, caring for his home, being grateful he still had one, taking on remodeling projects for his wife, and photographing the beautiful plants and creatures at the Preserve. Ironically, had he continued working in the construction industry, he and his wife would have not been able to afford the quality of labor he now performed in their home. Significantly, home became even more beautiful as a result of the loving simplicity they created with his custom hand craftsmanship. And, amazingly, the photography of the Builder became a new passion, as did viewing the eagles at the Preserve.

Still, at times, the Builder's bike rides were an immense part of what sustained him. And, every chance she got, his wife the Teacher joined him. Like the eagles they encountered, the Builder and Teacher were a team that loved each other. They knew that regardless of the challenges that lay ahead of them, they were mated for life. Together, they soared in the sunlight and soft breeze. As they biked, they talked about any and everything, making plans to stay healthy and grow old together. They both knew their lives were as fragile as any others during the recession. The Teacher was near the end of her time working with a small group of people who functioned from values she couldn't influence or abide; she had difficult work issues of her own. She and the Builder knew she would leave a position she had loved in spring of 2012. Although she would miss teaching students and working with other colleagues, she would not miss arguing with a small group that wanted something different than what she valued for her life. And at almost sixty years old, she wasn't ready to retire nor was she likely to be hired anywhere a younger candidate might apply. Like the Builder, she was not only losing her income, she was losing access to a line of meaningful work she loved. Teaching had been a means of contributing valuable skills and knowledge to others. She was a teacher of ethics in a time when ethics are increasingly fragile, and in a time when many people seem willing to compromise ethics in order to survive. Ironically, throughout history unethical people have used the times as an excuse for compromising ethics and values that they probably never embraced. Paradoxically, conceding one's ethical position in order to get along with others often threatens one's own survival as well as the survival of the others. The Preserve was a wonderful reminder of how people and other species can honor ethical contracts that benefit each other.

And so, the Builder and Teacher remained grateful. They smiled and spoke with many people they met along their rides. Among the folks they met was the Painter, a retired military man whose wife had passed away only a couple of years before. He too was a lover of eagles and, as would happen to an eagle, he missed his lifelong mate. In the past the Painter and his wife had observed the species in many different places. And, since he lived within a few miles of the Preserve, it was only natural that he would volunteer on his days off from painting. It was also only natural that the County would provide the Preserve, in the hands of the Painter, a sighting scope that would assist visitors in observing the young birds as it helped him to overcome his grief, share his knowledge and envision a future for eagles. The passersby were only too happy to join him as they longed to glimpse the majesty of two bald eagles, something they seldom imagined they would ever do. This was precisely the way that the Painter met the Builder and the Teacher. For each of these observers, the Preserve was becoming more sacred, a treasured and meaningful home that was bigger than their own nests. It became a place where they could soar above the mundane and recognize their freedom and vulnerability in a timeline of majesty. Watching eagles often quickly reminded them that one can rise above the difficulties that are inevitable in life. In the grand scheme of things, this is an important skill as human lives are really very short.

One day, as the Builder and the Teacher were biking through the trails, they spotted a distressed cormorant lying in the path. Quickly, they stopped, took a beach towel from the Teacher's bike-basket, and carefully moved the bird out of the pathway of humans. They examined it as best they could, and noted it had a deep wound where its wing joined the breast of its body. The bird was so weak and fragile that it did not even put up a fight. As the Teacher calmed the animal, the Builder rode off to find help. Fortuitously, he encountered Tom, a volunteer, and the two of them returned. The three caretakers soothed the creature as best they could while they waited for a vet to arrive, but alas, it was no use. Later, Tom buried the bird in its Ron-John's beach towel shroud and in a place of honor befitting its life in the Preserve.

Cormorants are normally a species that lives in and off of Florida bays and inlets. They are known for having a sharp hooked bill about 3-4 inches long that is used for catching live fish. The fact that this creature was willing to allow three locals to assist it in its struggle to survive meant it was in a desperate situation. Thereafter, every time Tom, the Builder and the Teacher saw each other on the path they knew they were all bird-and-critter lovers. They had been transformed as members of a sacred community joined by ritual, interdependence and love of the land. Their cormorant interaction had become the basis for the bird lovers to realize they were united in stewardship; they were all in for the duration of their time at the preserve. And, it was a foreboding of many lessons, 'presents' from birds yet to come.

Another local who frequented the Preserve was a retired Nurse who had dedicated much of her life to caring for others. She lived alone, with the exception of her dog, Angel, who had been acquired from a rescue shelter in early 2008. Angel had survived a hurricane in another Gulf State. She was healthy, strong, and tremendously grateful to her master who treated her as she deserved. Together they took daily walks in the Preserve that had so conveniently opened around the same time they had found each other. Angel and her master got to know many of the locals, any who were gracious enough to greet them and recognize the love they both had to share. It was only logical that they, the Painter, the Builder, the Teacher, the Ranger, Tom and others would all grow to become the eagle watchers that frequented and loved the preserve.

Word travelled fast about the lovely Preserve that seemed to quietly invite the community to enjoy its natural hospitality. And, as visitors and locals learned of its benefits, the community continued to grow. They came with their fishing rods and kayaks. They appeared with cameras and binoculars. They came by roller blade, bicycle, running shoes and sandals. And within a short period of time, the quiet community learned to distinguish the sound of the belly whop of a mullet. They appreciated the giggling voices of the ospreys. They were in awe of the whistling trill of the conversations of eagles. They knew they had lots to learn and they knew that they were home.

# Chapter 5 – Be It Ever So Humble...

A lone adult eagle in early December 2010, near where the tree came down

There is no place like home! And, in the early fall of 2010, the pair of young eagle parents began to settle into what they clearly believed was a well-made nest, their Florida winter home, in an Australian pine tree. With a few simple modifications, they easily retrofitted last year's accommodations to withstand this season's mating ritual, egg incubation and anticipated eaglet nursery. Diligently, when the young adult male first arrived, he immediately began preparing to impress his bride. Back and forth he flew, carrying fresh twigs, greens and sprigs to make the nest perfect for his mate's homecoming, perfect for their offspring to be born.

The locals caught glimpses of his labor. And as he flew by, they were in awe of his proud process. He gathered pine branches and other foliage to reinforce the nest infrastructure and make his family comfortable. It was obvious that he knew the nest would have to be strong enough to hold not only him, but his spouse and two to three young ones that would likely incubate at the beginning of winter. If all went well, they would hatch and spend their first months in the nest in the early spring. True that the eaglets would start out as small funny looking creatures with full-size beaks and claws that would make them seem awkward, top-heavy and clumsy at first. But within about two months, they would mature to full growth. And, by mid-spring the nest would need to be sturdy enough to hold the equivalent of four to five adults, as well as the groceries essential for a growing family to thrive.

Clearly, the adult male was making every attempt to prepare the nest for his life partner, whom he revered and treated as his equal, to take her place beside him high above all other creatures in the food chain along the Gulf, except of course for their own majestic family. Father eagle was ready for the family's most important adventure. Soon, he and his bride would begin the sacred rituals that would keep their family alive. Indeed, upon her arrival, the Mother eagle instinctively knew she was welcome, loved, appreciated and honored. Almost instantly the pair settled in for the six-month Florida winter season.

Each day they soared through the sky, hunting, fishing and enjoying each other's company. It was clear they sensed the crisp cool change in the air; that they had the awareness that soon it would be cool enough for them to begin laying eggs and then the incubation process. What a treat for the locals below, as they observed the eagles in flight! The birds attracted their undivided attention. People stopped biking; they ceased skating and paused hiking to catch a peek. Some even pulled the buds out from their ears. It was common to hear, "Look! Eagles are up there!"

It was normal to share updates, "They're re-building their nest. Look there! Do you see them? I think they're up in that pine."

As for the birds, well, they were like unaffected movie stars. They soared and glided. They were even observed mating in the Long Leaf pines on more than a few occasions. Then one day the winds changed. The eagles' blissful existence was terminated by a terrible storm that literally rocked their world. The tropical storm pummeled their nest. Rains came in torrents and the winds battered and blew the tree. All night the nest was pelted with buckets of icy rainwater during the cold and nasty squalls. Sure enough, early that next chilly December morning, the Ranger noticed that the old Australian pine, previously perceived by humans as just an invasive species, had come down. Although the eagles' nest was still intact, the tree's demise meant that the birds' (and the people's) hopes for a clutch of eggs that season were dashed. They had no place to lay eggs. The eagles had no place to raise their young.

During the next few days the eagles scuttled for basic shelter. They had survived the worst of the storm, but for about a fortnight they perched together, forlornly, on a human-made structure that had been created for ospreys. It was clear they were mourning the passing of their season. It was evident they knew if they didn't act swiftly and create a new nest, they would vanish as well. Like so many locals, the eagles had experienced their own form of foreclosure. They had experienced a tragedy, but they weren't about to give up. Unlike most humans, the eagles' instincts didn't allow for the luxury of self-pity. Part of the reason for their survival is their resilient attitude and a spirit that is truly amazing. Within a few days the pair was again busy, preparing lodging to shelter them as hopeful parents of a new clutch of eggs before the short, but bitter cold winter that would follow.

As the locals continued to watch, they saw the eagles in a new light. It was true. That winter there was no clutch of eagle eggs, but the couple found a way to survive. Through the crisis, they seemed to draw strength from each other and they lived up to their regal reputation. Somehow, the way the eagles managed their crisis caused some of the locals to begin reframing their own difficult situations. People enduring tough times seemed to see those times and themselves a little differently. All eyes were on the eagles as mentors who demonstrated exemplary survival skills to humans who needed to be reminded of the same.

The humans began to carefully "consider the birds of the air" (Matthew 6:26, NIV). They realized these birds were communicating important lessons. Like many humans who were now visiting the Preserve, things had not turned out like they had planned that winter. So they grieved on a vacant osprey nest, but only for a short time. The eagles took their place as role models in a time when talk is cheap. Their actions were far more powerful than any of the humans' words. The birds were no longer lofty movie stars; they had become local heroes. By the end of the season the birds had built yet another nest. It was strong and sturdy, big enough to house them and their offspring in the coming months. The eagles knew when they migrated in the early summer of 2011 that they had a nest to return to. They ensured they were prepared for mating season when they came 'home' in the fall.

# Chapter 6: The Eagles in History and Myth

The Preserve eagles grieving on an osprey platform shortly after their nest-home was lost in a windstorm

Throughout the ages, humans have had an affinity for eagles. Certainly one reason people have been so intrigued by these impressive birds is that humans have always wanted to fly and eagles have clearly been revered as masterful leaders in flight. Every culture has depicted earthbound human-like figures with eagle-like wings. In Greek mythology, Icarus, the son of the architect Daedalus, flew too close to the sun and the wax that was used to attach wings to his body as a means to escape from his earthly prison melted, thereby causing the captivated boy to plummet to his death (Daedalus and Icarus, 2012). Nike, the winged Greek goddess of victory, is one of the most frequently depicted deities on coins, as statuary and in paintings. It was rumored that she was close with the gods Athena and Zeus and that she soared above battle fields rewarding warriors for their courage and victory (Nike, 2012). Perseus, in his winged sandals, is reputed to have slain Medusa when no other hero was able to achieve such a daunting feat. Legend states that he carried her head in a bag and flew to his escape (Perseus, 2012). And Mercury, often described as a god who moved with the swiftness afforded by having wings on his feet, was nothing less than a messenger of the gods (Littleton, 2002).

Many references to eagles and the God of Abraham abound in the Bible too. In Deuteronomy, as Moses was attempting to lead his people in the desert, he sang a descriptive story of deliverance: "[God] shielded him and cared for him; he guarded [Jacob] as the apple of his eye, like an eagle that stirs up its nest and hovers over its young, that spreads its wings to catch them and carries them aloft" (Deuteronomy 32:11 NIV). In Isaiah it is written that "...those who hope in the Lord will renew their strength. They will soar on wings like eagles; they will run and not grow weary, they will walk and not be faint." (Isaiah 40:31, NIV). And in Psalms, King David praises the Lord "who satisfies your desires with good things so that your youth is renewed like the eagle's." (Psalms 103:5, NIV).

Eagles and other feathered creatures figure prominently in cultural history and mythology throughout the world. In Egypt Herodotus recorded that an eagle-like Phoenix produced the sun god. There was never more than one Phoenix alive at a time and it was rumored that the bird was capable of setting fire to its self and that it then could be reborn from its own ashes (Littleton, 2002, p. 30). In many Native American belief systems, sky spirits have inhabited "the circle of heaven and Thunderbirds or sky-dwellers are imbued with great power" (Littleton, 2002, p. 492-493). Totem poles, regalia, and other artifacts are decorated with winged people and eagle feathers and beaks adorn head-dresses reminiscent of splendid creatures of the sky. In some Native American tribal traditions, the term *season of eagles* is symbolic for a time when one chooses to use one's will and power in the world (RavenWing, 2000).

In fact, eagles are still often attributed with traits that include "great strength, vision, power, loyalty, will, beauty, spiritual achievement" (see Arcovio [1993], 2009). And truth be told, people are primarily earthbound without modern technology, but if we are open-minded, we can still learn many things from eagles. Some of the lessons the eagles taught the people at the Preserve during the winter of 2010 pertained to amazing partnerships. The adult eagles prepared to share parenting responsibilities, even before their young were eggs; after eggs were laid, both dad and mom sat on them as they were incubating. Both parents hunted for food and both eagles, as a team, proved they were adept at multiple types of problem-solving.

When the Australian pine tree fell and the eagles' nest came down, they stopped to grieve for a short time, but then the birds continued to work together. They were realists, optimists whose labor was shared equitably and fairly. They knew their survival was contingent on working together. So, the birds regained focus and demonstrated their ability to devise visionary, creative solutions. The eagles were committed to their family and their survival. They did not spend any unnecessary time sitting around and complaining. They had a life to plan and as a result, they showed the humans that they were a pair of amazing teachers. The lessons had begun!

# Chapter 7 – Envisioning a Future

The adult pair during mating season fall 2011

By spring 2011 it was time for the eagle pair to migrate away from Florida, just as it was for many of the people who frequented the Preserve. The birds had not had a clutch of eggs during the winter and the locals who had been watching them realized that the disturbance of the eagles' nest by the storm had disrupted their mating process. Still, the birds had set up housekeeping in a suitable tree, stayed together in their loving relationship and waited patiently; and for whatever reason, they did not lay eggs that year. Now and then the two juveniles from the previous year were occasionally spotted in the Preserve and in springtime they moved on with Mom and Dad. The locals wished them all farewell and hoped they would return once again in autumn.

By spring 2011, the numbers of visitors and volunteers at the Preserve had also continued to grow exponentially. University students and professors studied the plants and fisheries. Volunteers of all ages, shapes and sizes pulled out invasive Brazilian Pepper plants and other species deemed weeds that were constantly trying to take root. Tourists enjoyed low-impact environmental activities and entrepreneurs rented bicycles and kayaks to passersby who wanted to experience the Preserve in ways that they otherwise could not engage with it. Stakeholders of all walks of life attempted to restore the Preserve to its natural habitat. The once disturbed tropical farmland continued to flourish and become a refurbished coastal habitat where humans and animals alike appreciated the splendor and abundance of their wonderful Eden.

When the eagle pair returned in autumn 2011, Dad first in late August and Mom about a week after, right around Labor Day, the birds had become somewhat legendary. In fact, the eagles had become so popular that they decided it was in their best interests to move. Clearly, for the past few years the birds had had a vision for their life in the Preserve, but now they had to modify it. They had to get their vision for the immediate future right before settling in for the winter and beginning their mating rituals. It seemed as though they had vowed that this year there would be no interruption in the expansion of their family. This powerful team was determined to be successful in their mission.

At first, the locals were concerned – as it seemed that the eagle couple had become elusive. After the previous difficult winter, and now with increased numbers of visitors to the preserve, some locals were afraid the birds had decided to move on. The Builder, the Painter and the Teacher learned that one of the main difficulties American Bald eagles often have is finding a place to live in such an overpopulated society (American Bald Eagle Information, 2012). Eagle survival is still threatened by increases in human population and consumption; generally, the birds are threatened by humanity's need for more in a world that is enough.

That fall it quickly became clear that, like the other locals who had stayed in the area despite population increases, the eagle pair had found another Australian pine tree home in a prime location that afforded a view of the entire preserve. From where the eagles planned to build their nest they could see the Preserve's wonderfully engineered waterways where the mullet and red fish were frequently seen jumping. They could also view a dead end street not frequently traveled by humans. Once again, the eagles began to construct a nest that would be strong enough to support a healthy family, be large enough for their mating rituals, and durable enough to last for multiple generations of egg clutches and eaglet-toddlers. Though most of the locals did not know where the birds had gone, one day they revealed their strategy. The Builder, while riding his bike, saw them flying, carrying twigs and greenery to the new location. Without a word to anyone else, he stealthily followed them – and they let him!

Perhaps it was irony that the Builder had achieved the status of Eagle Scout as an adolescent; perhaps it was both his and the birds' destiny. In any case, it was a consecrated moment, a beginning of many lessons and the eagles seemed willing to let the Builder in on observing them. They seemed to realize that he, like them, had been through a rough time. They also seemed to know that he was no threat to them. He needed to learn what they could teach. The eagles also seemed to know that the Builder would only share information about how to reach their location with people who would respect them, revere them, and want to learn the lessons only the eagles knew.

There! Just ahead! In a stand of pines that would shelter a family in storms, in a less traveled area fit for a king and queen, was the makings of a new nest. For weeks, the Builder, the Rangers (formerly Tom and the Ranger), the Painter and the Teacher watched attentively as the eagles went about collaborative nest construction in their typical indomitable and fastidious manner. It was clear that the birds had learned from experience. It was also clear that they had no intention of letting anything or anyone defeat them. The watchers observed in awe as they began to perceive clearly just how eagles had earned their fame.

From the promontory of the new nest, the eagles could easily discern who was approaching their lair. They could identify enemies, allies, and tourists who might be curious or express ill-intent. They could not have selected a better location to start a family, to lay a new clutch of eggs at the dawn of the winter that was to come. By the beginning of October they began to settle in and during October and November there were frequent sightings of the eagles behaving as lovers. Throughout the Preserve their legendary status continued to grow. Locals and tourists alike paused just to get a glimpse of them. The eagles were beginning to be symbols of the Preserve; they were a visible manifestation of hope for the environment, the times, and the people who were privileged to be watching them thrive.

By Thanksgiving the excitement had spread. Like loyal citizens who revere their monarchs, the people at the Preserve watched and awaited the arrival of the eagle couple's heir. Daily, the Builder and the Painter – one on bicycle with binoculars, with camcorder and scope in his pack, the other in all-terrain-vehicle (ATV) with tripod/scope – exchanged data about the progress of the eagles. They shared copious notes with the Rangers and the developing group of stakeholders. Each day they updated the Teacher. Everyone had the wellbeing of the eagle family on their gratitude list for the holiday. It was clear that the eagles had become leaders of the roost. Fervently, locals followed their activities to learn anything and everything about them that they could. In some respects, people's conversations became more like the song of Moses – cheering the eagles on to their promised land, but knowing that humans are generally confined to the earth. Or are we? Somehow, the eagles inspired the locals so they felt like they could soar.

Chapter 8 – Preparing for the Ultimate Mentor Experience

An adult eagle preparing to lead the next generation

Although humans are primarily 'earth bound', the principal goal of each of us is to live up to, or soar to, our potential. For many reasons, achieving human potential is far from easy. Everyone has to overcome a unique set of obstacles in order to achieve his or her personal best. And, some people say that far too many humans find excuses or do not even try to live up to their potential; many humans seem to lack focus and simply drift through life from distraction to distraction.

Indeed, living up to one's potential can be even more difficult if a person does not realize any appropriate role models in the immediate environment. Contemporary every day heroes are sometimes hard to find, so many humans settle for imitating lifestyles of celebrities or trendsetters instead, again causing them to drift from trend to trend, distraction to distraction, and the possibility of an unsatisfying existence devoid of the intent to soar to one's potential.

On the other hand, eagles are amazingly focused role models who spend much of their lives demonstrating what it means to literally soar to one's potential, despite tremendous obstacles. Their behavior is quite intentional. In fact, the birds focus most of their energy on ensuring that the next generation sees, and therefore knows, how to achieve each step of the 'soaring to one's potential' process. These birds are skilled and articulate mentors.

As we have observed in the previous chapters, from the beginning of their long-term relationship, eagles work as an egalitarian pair, building and maintaining a proper nest for purposes of keeping their eggs safe and secure during the incubation process. Both male and female eagles share incubating the eggs, ensuring they are warm and guarded from predators. After the eggs hatch, a rigorous training program begins. The youngsters must be taught to fly and land, to hunt and fish, and to stay safe from the dangers around them. Like humans, baby eagles even have to be taught how to feed themselves.

Many of the ways in which eagles teach their young to live up to their potential are nothing short of quite remarkable. In fact, early eagle parenting has been carefully outlined in sermons such as one delivered by Pastor Kraig Pullam. Pastor Pullam's sermon discusses eagle parenting skills in a way that can easily be translated to mentoring, coaching and developing followers as a servant leader. What differentiates a servant leader, or servant led group, from others is the intent and motivation of the leader. Like an eagle parenting its young, a servant leader lives to serve first and, as a result, the eagle and 'eaglet' both emerge as competent, capable leaders. Further, as a result of their interactions, the 'eaglet' is more likely to be motivated to serve and lead the next generation. Most other types of leaders are motivated to lead, rather than serve, first (see Greenleaf, 1970). This one factor makes all the difference in how they see themselves, and in how they relate to those who follow them.

According to Pastor Pullam, Moses' song in Deuteronomy was meant to cheer others on to deliverance despite Moses' divine knowledge that he would not complete the journey to the Promised Land. In essence, he too engaged in servant leadership designed to ensure that his people would thrive and God would be glorified. Pastor Pullam likened the scripture to eagle parents teaching their young to succeed in a harsh environment where survival is difficult.

Broadly speaking, the five-part development process communicated by the adult eagles and outlined in Pullam's sermon is easily discernible. Its steps are:

1) The eagle disturbs its young

Some sources say that eagles build their nests so that disturbing their young is inevitable. As part of the construction process, the eagles input hard, sometimes sharp, strong limbs and other foundation materials that hold the bottom of the nest together and keep it strong, so the nest is able to withstand tests of weather and time. It is important to remember, the first nest that the Preserve eagles built endured. It was the tree that blew down in a wind storm, as it had been treated as an invasive species by well-meaning local people who didn't realize eagles were trying to make a home in the pine. Also, eagles don't typically live in their nests, except when they are in the early parenting process. The birds use their nests for egg incubation and early child rearing. They build the nests as high up as possible to protect their young from most predators. After the eaglets learn to fly, the family spends most of its time in the air, demonstrating exceptional abilities and causing everyone around to look up in awe.

When the foundation of the nest has been laid, the multi-faceted construction process continues; eagles cover the rugged floor with pine sprigs and branches, moss, peat and greenswards, softer grasses and greenery that are cushion-like and fill in gaps, cementing the footing and providing a comfortable floor for developing eagles and, at times, their dinner-prey. Upper levels of the nest are where eagle feathers, down and the softest materials insulate and support the babies. And, as the infants grow in size, their own weight makes them feel the presence of harsher materials under the feather cushion. The larger the eaglet becomes, the more he or she is inclined to feel uncomfortable. As the eaglet grows, and they grow quickly, their parents regularly communicate, both verbally and non-verbally, that soon it will be time to soar. The eaglets reach adult size in a matter of a few awkward weeks and the design of the nest encourages them to literally try their wings. Similarly, when developing people it is wise to ensure that the challenges provided for their development are appropriate for their stages of growth.

Just as Moses sang, "like an eagle that stirs up its nest" (Deuteronomy 32:11 NIV), young eaglets are encouraged to become independent by their own growth. Watching the Preserve eagle parents continue to build progressively better nests reminded the locals it is always important to do one's best (the birds did not know the first tree would not endure). It is not how many times life knocks us down, but how many times we get up and keep trying that matters. Even though the process of falling can be disturbing; it makes us stronger and can lead us to our destiny, our Promised Land. When helping to develop others it is important to realize they too will fall, but stumbles are often valuable learning experiences that can teach success in the developmental process.

*2)* The adult eagle draws near to its eaglets

Adult eagles communicate encouragement to their eaglets physically, through touch, and vocally, through speech. After an eaglet hatches and during its ongoing maturation the parents, together or separately, speak to and nudge the child as part of its socialization. Great mentors also communicate encouragement to their charges. They sponsor them, introduce them to other 'eagles' and assist them in achieving their potential - just as the eagle parents literally draw near to encourage their young to fly and achieve other goals by cheering the eaglets on. Moses knew, the eagle parent "hovers over its young" (Deuteronomy 32:11 NIV), conceding that many tasks ahead of the eaglet are going to be tough. In fact, some sources say only about 40% of young bald eagles survive. The parents ensure the babies know they are there for them. They stay around to actively assist in teaching the young to fly, fish, hunt and do other essentials of a healthy growth process. Great mentors, like eagles, celebrate small wins with their charges. They review losses and integrate them as stepping stones in the developmental process.

By watching adult eagles with their young, the locals at the Preserve were reminded of the importance of sticking together. In fact, as time went on, they too drew closer as a community. And the people of faith within the community were reminded of the scripture's admonition to trust in the Lord who treats each one as the only one – the apple of God's eye – providing support as we attempt to soar and achieve our potential. This is great advice for mentors as well. Instead of comparing one 'eaglet' to another, it is wiser to compare each 'eaglet' to its self. That way, each eaglet can develop and be appreciated for his or her own unique combination of gifts, potential and performance.

*3)* The eagle parent demonstrates what is expected of the eaglet

Eagles are phenomenal role models for their young. Unlike many human parents or leaders, they do not subscribe to the theory of 'do as I say, not as I do'. Eagles show their young how to do everything necessary for them to thrive. As has been said, their authentic demonstrations of collaborative preparation are visible even before eaglets arrive. The couple acts as a unit, working together to build their nest. They share responsibilities and their prey (rewards). The parents demonstrate love and loyalty; they mate for life, and are partners, stakeholders and stewards in everything they do. Eagles socialize their young for months prior to letting the youngsters go out on their own. Youths are taught to tear their food, clean the nest, fly with the adults, migrate, and much more before they achieve independence. Servant leaders develop their followers similarly. They serve as powerful examples who model what is expected of their charges, in the true spirit of egalitarianism. Just as eaglets constantly see their parents as a team collaborating for the benefit of the unit, followers of servant leaders see their leaders as approachable role models. Both eagle parents and servant leaders shield their young and care for them. They want their charges to learn to soar so they can model the same ideals for the next generation of followers. The young are "…the apple of [the servant leaders'] eye, like an eagle that stirs up its nest and hovers over its young" (Deuteronomy 32:11).

Eagle parents know their children are reflections of their leadership, and they take every opportunity as a teachable moment in ongoing exemplary education for their young. For the locals, the eagle pair demonstrated that potential and performance are two vividly distinct phenomena. Potential is what people (or eagles) 'have' or can be, performance is demonstrated for the world to see. We exhibit who we are in the most difficult and wonderful moments of our lives, whether we realize it or not. Each decision affords us an opportunity to demonstrate behavior of an eagle, a turkey, or a vulture. Ultimately, the choices are up to us.

*4)* The eagle parents develop their young eaglets

Some eagle stories say the adults carry their young to great heights on their backs and then shake them off to teach the young to fly. According to the story Moses sings, the eagle "spreads its wings to catch the [eaglets] and carries them aloft" (Deuteronomy 32:11 NIV). This is similar to giving youngsters difficult, achievable challenges and then sticking around - sometimes out of sight of the new-be - to assist, guide and mentor them, but only as support is needed. This does not mean the adults coddle the eaglets, nor does it mean a leader should do a follower's tasks. It does mean that both eagles and servant leaders ensure that their 'eaglets' have the freedom and support to make decisions, mistakes and victories. The novices also have the assurance that their leaders remain available to assist when the 'eaglet' requests their help, which is inevitable. This stage of development entails watching so the 'eaglet' does not get harmed or destroy itself in the learning process. It involves being an approachable and understanding mentor.

For the locals, the community they were developing was rapidly becoming a support system wherein everyone was respected for his or her unique contribution and creativity. The locals were learning to protect each other, the Preserve, and the eagles by acting as stewards and staying close, but out of the eagles' (and each other's) way unless help was needed.

*5)* Eagle parents are there to deliver their young

The end of Pastor Pullam's sermon, the aforementioned Bible scripture in Deuteronomy, and the story of the Preserve eagles as parents pertains to deliverance. If an eaglet is in danger, according to Pullam and the Bible, the parent swoops down, lifts the child up, "and carries them aloft" (Deuteronomy 32:11 NIV). As an eaglet is socialized and learns to make decisions, its parents observe. They stand back, near enough to intervene if and when they are asked (or needed) to help. The eagle parent appears to have learned, probably from its own instincts and socialization, when it is appropriate to insert its presence into the youngster's experiences. Similarly, the locals learned important lessons about boundaries - between each other, between themselves and the birds, the Preserve, and eagles/Nature in a grander context. The locals were continuously learning how to be protective, without inhibiting or endangering, the eagle family's environment. This involved exercising common sense, humility and respect for creatures both similar and dissimilar to themselves. It was multi-level demonstration of servant leadership exemplified by all of the stakeholders, eagle and human alike.

On Christmas Eve, 2011, the adult eagles who had carefully and lovingly prepared a place for their offspring, the birds who had been so patiently waiting to be parents, laid one egg in the nest that would serve as their home for the next few months. While the others were at church, or spending time with their loved ones, a single local, the Painter, was there to observe from his scope. The gifts that emerged from observing the baby eagle that would hatch a little over a month later, and be socialized by amazing parents over the next few months, will grace the Preserve and be shared by the community for many years to come. The egg represented another phase of shared responsibilities for the parents. It symbolized an array of other relationships; each of the locals involved in the eaglet observation became a partner in its well-being. This was going to be a very merry Christmas.

The eagle parents and their eaglet had simply communicated their vision to the locals, and the locals had all begun to understand. The birds were the impetus for friendships and new beginnings, their own as well as others with the extended family that had chosen to embrace them. It was a new time, a new beginning of teachable moments unlike any the community members had ever experienced. It was doubtful the eagles had ever experienced anything like this either.

As the adult Preserve eagles settled in for the winter of 2011, they began to demonstrate eagle superb parenting strategies, just as those described in the sermon, to anyone astute enough to observe them. This is not to say the lessons the eagles' teachings would culminate in humans literally learning to fly, but people who watched closely could easily see how eagles earned a reputation for strength and power that expands ages and cultures. Many of the Preserve watchers were lifted up, reminded daily to 'soar' as the best people they could be, by observing the rituals and processes of these magnificent, caring raptors. The eagles served as role models and servant leaders. In a world where talk is often cheap, their actions spoke more powerfully than most any human words.

# Chapter 9 – Life Lessons From the Perspective of a Baby Eagle

Mother eagle nurturing the baby at about one month old

For the first few weeks of 2012, all that was visible in the eagles' nest was one adult, sometimes two, staying close to each other, to their egg, and to their temporary home. The locals learned that the resplendent young parents dutifully shared all of the burdens of infant care, including incubating the egg, keeping it warm, and keeping each other well fed, unafraid and loved. At least one adult bird was visible in the nest at all times, but sometimes observers caught glimpses of the other eagle preparing a picnic or treating his or her spouse to time alone on a higher perch where the bird needing a reprieve could feast and relax in solitude. Each adult seemed to recognize and respect the other's need for time away from the uncomfortable task of sitting on an egg that was not expected to hatch for about 35 days (American Bald Eagle Information, 2012).

Finally, at the end of the first week in February, the egg hatched! Out came an uncoordinated fuzzy ball of down that could hardly hold up its big giant full-sized beak. The eaglet's head primarily consisted of two-soon-to-be-piercing eyes and a huge beak from which emanated an inelegant high-pitched squawk. However, as soon as baby made its appearance in the nest, a new level of activity began both in the nest and the Preserve. It was clear that the eaglet's parents intended to waste no time empowering their young. It was also clear that the locals, unlikely adopted god-parents, wanted to learn all they could of the baby's 'firsts' – from a safe, respectable legal distance, that is! They knew that even though eagle learning experiences were now regularly in session, they still had to remain at least 500 feet away from the tree that housed the beautiful protected nest. Eagles are still, necessarily, protected by strict federal laws, and eaglets are also protected by strong and powerful guardians. The locals did not want to interfere, but they wanted to observe it all!

During the first few months of the eaglet's life, she (who the locals named Maggie, short for Magnificence) learned many life-changing lessons. Some of the lessons the parents taught the eaglet were suitable for the willing locals as well. They included:

Lesson #1: Always remember, if you were intended to be an eagle that is what you are! Why would you want to try to be anything else?

Eagles never forget who or whose they are, no matter what. They never represent themselves as anything or anyone that they are not. Nor are they envious of the talents of herons, ospreys, egrets, hawks or vultures. They don't engage in the manipulative hijinks of distractions such as buzzards, coyotes, or other such misguided critters. They have no need or desire to derail other birds from living up to their highest potential. In fact, these ideas are so human that they would *never* even cross an eagle's mind. This knowledge is critical for the survival of eagles. It can be equally important for humans to remember too. After all, each of us is a unique creation, a one-of-a-kind combination of talents that, if we don't focus on and develop, will be missing from the greater tapestry of life.

One day in mid-March, the Teacher was biking with the Builder. She had been preparing an important project with students. A colleague known for her interference and for being a bit of a control freak, was trying to take credit for the project at the last moment, rather than letting the students learn what they set out to learn, rather than letting them see they were on the way to developing their soaring potential. As the Teacher and Builder biked past the eagles' nest, they discussed the situation. Then they saw Mother Eagle and child relaxing. Just as the bikers left the nest area, the Teacher spotted Father Eagle at the end of an open field. He sat high atop an African Orchid tree, alone, savoring a fresh caught mullet and, clearly, enjoying his feast.

Suddenly, seemingly out of nowhere, a band of turkey vultures zoomed in. They dive-bombed the eagle, attempting to fluster him so he'd drop his meal and they could quickly scoop it up. They swooped and circled, spiraled up and plummeted down, each time moving closer, as close as they dared mob the noble raptor and his meal. In a little while, Father Eagle looked up, but only ever so briefly. He was cool and calm, and then he returned to the task at hand. There he remained, enjoying his fish amidst the chaos that was the lifestyle of the ravenous vultures, these scavengers of the air that were trying to distract him so they could steal his catch!

In a split second, as the eagle evaluated the situation, he seemed to say – without making a single sound, "I'm an eagle. You're turkey vultures. At best, you will enjoy my droppings. At worst, you will get nothing. In any case, you'll have to focus your ineffective distractions on another target, at another time and in another place. No one fears your chaos here". The Teacher and Builder turned and stared at each other. Yes, they had both seen it! They recognized the singularity of focus, the vision of the eagle, and the honor with which he continued his task without giving in to the vultures. His demeanor was indicative of so many events that happen in the course of human lives. Yes, only a moment before the teacher had been distracted, talking on her cell phone, something she did not often do during bike rides. She'd been concerned about protecting a students' project from a human-turkey-vulture and, more specifically, she had been troubled by the actions of an adult who had tried to derail a project and a student with whom she had been collaborating for months.

The project disrupter was a lot like the turkey vulture, attempting to dive bomb, to mob the work team, but undoubtedly she was only capable of handling scraps that the teacher and students might 'drop' along the way. The eagle had offered the gift of a teachable moment that demanded to be shared with others. He had reminded the Teacher: no one can take one's power (or one's 'catch') unless it is given to them. And, importantly, although only an eagle is an eagle, we each have unique talents. Turkey vultures can try, but they will never soar to the heights that eagles, eaglets, or well-intentioned talented humans can attain. The eagle, unlike so many human beings, was quite sure of his identity – he knew exactly who and whose he was and the turkey vultures were just a distraction. They were reminders of what he was not, and had no other function in his life. The eagle did not take time to respond to them; he did not lose his focus. His energy was intentionally dedicated to the task at hand and to developing his eagle potential.

<u>Lesson #2: No matter how many others believe in you, you cannot fly until you believe that you can.</u>

One day the Teacher and Builder biked over to the nest. There, to their surprise, was Mother Eagle and the baby. It appeared the parent had just fed the youngster and that she and her child were engaged in an argument. The Mother was making agitated noises at the eaglet; almost as though she was trying to convince the child it was time to fly, time to believe that the young eaglet could do it. In response, the eaglet screeched – as if to say, "No, I'm not ready! I'm too afraid and the drop from this tree is such a long way down!" Whether the eaglet <u>could</u> have flown at that time was a moot point. Its unwillingness to try meant the child was confined to the nest. No matter how much the parent cheered the baby on, flight was not to happen. Baby Maggie did not believe she could do it and so, no matter what anyone else told her, she was undoubtedly right.

This is so true for humans too. No matter how many friends, colleagues, family members or other supporters one has, if one does not believe in his or her self, nothing is going to happen. A person who believes he or she cannot perform at the level of their potential is absolutely right – as long as they don't try. As was stated, performance and potential are two different things and if a person is convinced that they cannot perform, their potential remains untapped. A person or eagle will remain confined to an ever increasingly uncomfortable nest. In the case of the eagle the ramifications become clear more quickly: the eaglet will eventually be left alone to fly or die. In the case of the human it is not as obvious, but ultimately the same final result. A person who does not attempt to live up to his or her potential never truly lives – and there are many around us. As they sit uncomfortably in their nests, they screech at the rest of humanity, sort of like the turkey vultures mobbing the feasting eagle. Some of the locals stood in awe of this lesson. That big eagles' nest no longer looked so attractive!

<u>Lesson #3: Even if you fall out of the nest, don't panic. Remember you know how to survive!</u>

One Sunday, in late April, there was a big rain storm. The winds blew and the rains were torrential. All of the locals were concerned about the eagles (no doubt, thinking of them in less powerful human terms). No one was biking or walking through the Preserve that day. Even if the humans had been near the eagles, what could they have done? The next day, the Builder was babysitting his grandson. He loaded the four-year old with him in the car. The two drove to the nest three times, but couldn't find hide or feather of any of the birds. The Builder worried aloud,

"Did the baby fall out of the nest? And if so, would she be able to survive?" He had heard frightening stories, and he had been learning more about eagles from a variety of other sources.

In many accounts from the locals, it was said that eaglets that fell out of their nests were not likely to survive. At the end of the day the Builder returned for the fourth time, this time with the Teacher in tow. He, the Painter and other members of the eagle watching community had set up a phone tree so that if any one person saw an eagle, the others would soon learn how they were. Although no one vocalized it, the locals all feared that the eaglet might have met with her demise. They were apprehensive that coyotes and other species might be dining on the beautiful young and surely frightened, inexperienced young bird.

The next day, Tuesday, the Builder and Teacher again rode bikes to the nest in the late afternoon. Sure enough, they spotted the eaglet! She was on top of a tree about 10 feet below her nest! She took flight, but couldn't gain the altitude to get back home. She didn't seem panicked, but it was clear she had been traumatized by the incident and she felt she knew her limitations. Her parents were near, but it was inevitable that the eaglet had to learn to fly. Mom and Dad could keep away her natural enemies, but sooner than later, Maggie would have to learn to survive in order to get home. She was now too big for them to carry. Likewise, human leaders, mentors and parents can only assist their followers so far. Ultimately, survival is contingent on not panicking, and on learning how to soar. There are times in life when we each 'fall out of the nest', but if we don't panic, we are far more likely to survive and make it home. We have to try our wings – to get back up and get strong.

Lesson #4: No matter what a coyote may tell you, the coyote is not your friend.

Each day, weather permitting, after Maggie was seen unable to get back to her nest, some of the locals biked, walked or drove in search of her. Each person was concerned that the eaglet would not be able to get back home and they all kept track of places where she'd been spotted, what she was doing, and if it appeared she was in imminent danger. One day the Builder spotted the young bird sitting on a power pole just west of her nest. Another day the Painter reported seeing her atop a berm that had been created just north of the nest. Each day, as locals expressed their concern for her welfare, they couldn't help but notice at least one set of coyote tracks, usually accompanied by scat droppings and other evidence that Maggie was being stalked by yet another observer who wasn't so well intentioned.

Each day, as the locals attempted to guard the eaglet, they paid careful attention to the tracks and droppings of the coyote. They looked for evidence of a struggle with young Maggie. The Painter said he had actually seen the coyote prowling near the berm where they both had been spotted. The locals all cared, and they worried; they hoped that Maggie would be able to discern that the coyote was not her friend. They knew her instincts were sound, even though her experience was limited. She had many well-meaning adults, including both of her parents, looking out for her, but ultimately Maggie herself would have to discern that the coyote was not her friend.

In life humans also occasionally attract 'coyotes'. In fact, some Native American folk lore still refers to coyotes as 'tricksters' who disguise themselves as friends when what they really want is to claim all that the eaglet, or novice person, has strived to achieve. And, some Native American traditions still view eagles as sacred creatures, "spiritual messengers" who liaise between heaven and earth (see Cultural Significance of the Bald Eagle). In this context, the coyote might be seen as the eagle's mortal enemy.

Thus, no matter what the coyote tried to tell the eaglet, she was protected. She appeared to be astute enough to realize he was not her friend. Her instincts convinced her that the coyote's actions spoke far louder than his 'words'. And, at the Preserve, for almost two weeks Maggie managed to avoid the mutt, sometimes with assistance from her parents, who kept close watch on her from above. Other times she was assisted by hawks, sea birds, humans or other creatures who warned her that he was too near. The locals watching Maggie grew ever more concerned that she might not be able to get back to the nest and that she was feeding on the ground in an area of the preserve where coyotes had been seen, but her instincts were clearly stronger than theirs. She might have been in jeopardy from time to time, but Maggie was healthy and she had the support of two wonderful mentors and a host of well-meaning locals. She had learned to trust her parents. More importantly, through their guidance, love and development, she was learning to trust herself. They had taught her about healthy relationships.

Her guides reinforced her choices and finally, she grew strong and resourceful enough to catch the right draft and go home. She flew up and into the nest, safe and sound, albeit a little flustered and disheveled. The coyote remained earthbound and disappointed; and she was safe in the nest. Maggie had not been fooled. Mom and Dad returned with a feast of fresh fish and the locals quietly celebrated down below. Humans can learn much from this prodigal eaglet. Often, we learn to trust the judgment of others more than our own instincts. We all need to believe in ourselves, rather than in coyotes who may try to trick us – and whose actions speak louder than words.

<u>Lesson #5: Remember to be grateful to your true supporters. You could not have accomplished your goals without them.</u>

It was Monday, May 14, precisely two weeks after she had been blown out of the nest by a windstorm when Maggie returned to her home. As quickly as she had flown out, the grateful eaglet put on a show for the locals. She flew high, swooping down, circling the nesting area and flawlessly landing on top of a tree about 20 feet away from her home. She began to 'talk', "Look at me! I can do it! I am safe, sound, and loved."

She communicated victory. "Look at me! I am home", she informed the supporters of her travels. "I am home and I am grateful to you. I drew strength from all of those who had faith for me."

Maggie sounded strong, as if she had found her voice and was ready to sing another chapter of her story. Surely she was thanking her supporters. There was no distress in her call.

Once again, Maggie was teaching the locals. She expressed gratitude for their assistance, but she was lucidly confident in her new found skills and achievements. Often, when people succeed, we can forget to thank those who have assisted us. Similarly, there is a fine distinction between assistance and control. The humans gained valuable insight from Maggie. Her gratitude in no way diminished her achievements. In fact, it made her stronger, more powerful, as she was capable of sharing credit for triumph – and there was surely enough to go around. As a result of her demonstration of shared leadership, Maggie had strengthened the community. At the same time, the locals were learning more about maintaining healthy boundaries so they could continue to observe this young eagle as she began to come of age. The locals were free to learn from the eagle family as long as they did not interfere with the lessons. Their learning was even more meaningful when they realized that Maggie's socialization process was theirs too, in a very different way. For that they were deeply grateful. Some things are meant to be beyond human control.

Lesson #6: Never stop learning. There is always more to know and the environment is constantly changing.

By Tuesday, the next day, Maggie was home in the nest, with her parents both flying in circles above her. They called to let her know how much fun they were having doing what they are intended to do.

"Come on, Maggie! Join us! This is what you were created to do. Come soar with us. Don't lose your momentum. You can reach up to 10,000 feet or more!"

It was clear that Maggie's parents had no intention of allowing her to rest on her laurels; she had only just begun some of her most important learning. Now that they knew she was safe, sound and successful, the lessons would escalate. In a few short months, Maggie's parents would need to teach their young beautiful eaglet to fly, and even more importantly, to land and take off again on a moment's notice. They would have to show her how to dive and fish, which undoubtedly looks easier than it is. They would teach this brilliant protégé how to fend in a constantly changing environment and, as part of that process they would prepare the young bird for a long and arduous flight. After all, the eagle family typically migrated for summer and they clearly expected Maggie to go too.

For now, Maggie flew to the top of a tree about 25 feet away from the nest. Although she was still a little too afraid to join her parents at first, everyone knew Maggie's continuous learning was inevitable. It was clear that whether she would be able to join her parents in advanced aspects of her training would ultimately define the quality of her life. As the locals observed her, many of them realized that due to the recession they too had had a reprieve. For now, they were safe from coyotes and vultures, but soon it would be time to get back into flight. We are all destined to soar and perform; and they all knew they could remember to soar. Otherwise, if humans don't soar, our potential is untapped and means little. Ultimately, the quality of our lives is contingent on whether we are willing to keep learning. And a large portion of our continuous learning is a matter of adjusting, and learning to be proactive in an ever-changing environment.

<u>Lesson #7: Keep the faith. You didn't make it this far to not continue to succeed.</u>

That same week there were several rainy and windy days. The locals knew that Maggie had been a bit traumatized by the weather and being blown her out of the nest only a few short weeks ago. From time to time, the Builder, Painter, Teacher and Rangers saw her hunkered down low in the nest, attempting to remain safe from the storms. She was almost full sized now and the nest must have been getting really uncomfortable. Mother and Dad eagle were also clearly tired, ready to get on with her training, and then on with their lives. They had to be getting weary of feeding someone whose growth was so dramatic, whose needs were demanding, and who was about the same size as them, but they remained steadfast in their goals. They were remarkable role models that remained committed to the development of the eaglet.

On one especially rainy and windy Wednesday, Maggie was not in the nest when the Builder and Teacher finally drove to see her late in the day. High winds, heavy rains and tornadoes had been reported during the previous evening and throughout the night. They were more than a little concerned, but of one thing they were sure: eagles can and will take care of themselves if we don't interfere.

Early the next day, when the Thursday sun shone briefly, the Teacher and Builder saw Dad eagle and Maggie busy chowing-down in the nest. Maggie was squealing, sharing her fears about flying in inclement weather. Dad stood between her and the locals as they videoed from afar. As he looked at the locals, it was clear he was a Dad comforting his daughter after the nasty storm the night before. He looked weary and the locals grasped that even these brilliant and powerful creatures must have fleeting moments when they just want to give up. It was evident that Dad eagle did not perceive either local as a threat; he seemed to realize they too were invested in the success of his young daughter. His pep talk to Maggie was palpable as Dad reminded her that the difference between survival and greatness is often not giving up.

"Press in and press on!" He seemed to impart the wisdom and courage that has distinguished champions from the mediocre throughout the ages. The humans were deeply humbled as they knew he was right.

Later, as the Builder and the Teacher biked along a trail, they saw Mother eagle too. She was busy catching a mullet and landed closer to the locals than they had ever seen. They stopped suddenly, quietly, to observe her, and to ensure she knew they would not interfere with her mission. In those brief, but precious moments, all three eagles were acutely aware that they had made it through the storms. Both the eagles and locals seemed to share the knowledge that they had been through storms, but for now, the worst was over. They each had faith in something larger than themselves and their connection assured them that neither of them had been brought this far to fail. They were destined to succeed and, in some way, their successes were linked together in an interdependence that was larger than any of them.

Lesson #8: Setbacks are just that. They might set you back, but then you carry on. Remember, you are an eagle. If necessary, refer to Lesson #1.

By the end of the week, the wet stormy weather began to subside. The sun was shining and summer seemed imminent. Locals and eagles alike began to celebrate the blue skies and warm weather so wonderfully typical during spring on the west coast of Florida. Each of them realized brighter days were ahead. They had all experienced setbacks, but as the eagles soared in the sky, now conducting regular flying lessons, the locals stood tall below. As often as they could manage, the Builder, the Painter and the Teacher visited the Preserve to celebrate the flights of the eaglet and the renewal of spring. They were sometimes joined by many others. Everyone seemed to share knowledge about special places where eagles could be viewed. And as the raptors soared in the sky, no one doubted that they were birds of distinction. It was clear beyond any shadow of a doubt, they were not buzzards, vultures, or crows – they were eagles. And somehow, the locals knew that this recognition was shared. In some small way, perhaps as the result of many small miracles, the locals had each become 'eagles' in their own rite too. After all, they too had experienced setbacks, but like the eagles, they were about to soar. They could not be kept on the ground and they would not be held down.

# Chapter 10 – When the Eaglet is Ready, the Teachers Will Appear

Maggie, as a young eaglet who could not yet fly home to the nest

By mid-April, just about everyone who regularly visited the Preserve knew something about the legendary family of eagles. People came from far and wide to enjoy the beauty of the place. Volunteers still picked weeds and continued with other improvements, but by now, spring was in the air and eagle flying lessons were regular occurrences. They were also taking on increasing importance. Those who knew anything at all about eagles were aware that soon Maggie and her family would leave them. However, before that could happen, young Maggie would have to become proficient at flying, and more importantly, at landing. She still had more to learn about fishing and hunting and there was more she needed to know about how to discern her friends from her enemies. She was learning all of these lessons, but at a time of increased activity in the preserve. As the weather continued to get balmier, more humans arrived each day. They brought their kayaks and fishing rods (also learning to fish), but for the most part, they were respectful and curious. They wanted to learn any and everything that the eagles were willing to teach them. Here are some of the later lessons that people of the Preserve were taught.

Lesson #9: Timing is important in life. Never fly in such a way that the wind will be against you if you can use it to your advantage; in the spirit of the famous old Irish prayer, 'May the wind always be at your back'.

As young Maggie became more adept at flying, she began to teach the locals many lessons. These included easy and not so easy ways to get back to the nest. One Friday, in mid-May, Maggie sat atop a dead tree with a perpendicular perch at its apex. She was well shielded from the fronds of the pines that surrounded the perch, but she appeared to be waiting when the Teacher and Builder biked by. When they stopped to observe her, she lowered her head, bowing regally as if signaling their presence and her desire to wish to acknowledge their admiration. After a few minutes the bicyclists hopped back on the road, pedaling swiftly, steadily toward the sheltered side of the Preserve where they could watch her more closely and she could feel free to demonstrate her skill. As they approached, Maggie called to them. She heralded their presence with her distinctively eagle trill. They watched as she flexed her muscular wings, stretching, greeting them and showing off ever so politely.

"Look what I can do now", she seemed to communicate. "Consider the majesty of the creature that perches above your head. I am strong, magnificent and yet mind-bogglingly gentle. I am the living being I was intended to be."

As the Builder and Teacher stood in awe, Maggie continued her airborne ballet, flexing, stretching and caressing the breezes on which she was so capable of soaring. Then, in an instant, she lifted up, turned, circled higher in the sky above them and swooped back toward her nest. As she glided in, they couldn't help but notice she was no longer a clumsy child; her landing was as natural as could be. She seemed to float into the nest where she made herself comfortable and settled in for a warm mid-morning nap. They knew that the opportunity to observe such a beautiful ritual was an honor. And they knew, in a few weeks this lesson, like so many others, would be a wonderful memory. Maggie, along with her parents, would be prepared to migrate on to their northern home. The locals knew that, through Maggie, they had received a sacred gift.

Lesson #10: Never, ever take watching eagles or other marvels of Nature for granted. Live within your means with a deep appreciation of everything that contributes to the quality of your life. You may find that you have more than you think you had.

Often we define wealth far too narrowly. This lesson considers the beauty of Nature that is all around us and that we have been entrusted with as stewards. On one spring day the Preserve was particularly active with human activity. As the Builder and the Teacher biked along the paths, the Ranger in a golf cart hailed them eagerly,

"Hey guys." He called. "Ahead, near the next bridge, there's a professional photographer taking pictures of our eagles!" And sure enough, there was.

The photographer glanced at the bikers as if they were intruders. They exchanged civil, yet disconnected 'hullos'.

"Are they all at home?" The teacher queried.

"Oh, is there more than one?" the photographer mumbled back.

"Yes, it's a family of three." the Builder and Teacher seemed to sing out in unison.

"Oh, didn't know…seems like only one of them is home." The photographer shot back, clearly nonplussed by their presence.

"Shall we go on?" The Teacher asked the Builder.

"I guess." He responded, not quite picking up on her uneasy insight that the preserve seemed a little crowded today.

As they glided on through the trails to the other side of the preserve, they chatted, discussing plans for the future weeks of summer, their travels and plans with friends. Suddenly, seemingly out of nowhere, another biker whizzed past them. He wore a helmet, synthetic bike shorts, and an expensive wicking shirt. His bike, which seemed to whoosh past, was top of the line, a racer – and he appeared to perceive himself in the same category as he almost ran the couple off the road.

"Hey! What are you doing?" The Teacher shouted as she stopped short, barely avoiding crashing into stickers in a ditch. The Builder, a sensitive soul, stopped too. He was troubled that she might have gotten hurt by his inattention, not realizing the Teacher again sensed that human invasion has been the traditional nemesis of bald eagles. Close, in a nest that could only protect her for a little while longer, was Maggie. The Teacher and the Builder knew that incivility would likely be the bane of the young eagle if she and her parents didn't migrate soon. Too many people were visiting the Preserve and forgetting, if they ever knew, that we are all called to be stewards of the earth in an I-thou relationship.

When they arrived beneath the nest, there was Maggie. She was peacefully preening and glanced their way. She put her head down as if to acknowledge them, but she did not speak. She was quiet, as if she too knew it was busy human-invasion-day at the lovely Preserve. She fussed with her nest, rearranging sticks as an adolescent girl might primp in her bedroom. She seemed to know it was wise to stay 'in' now, not exposing her inexperience to visitors who were not part of the close-knit community of the Preserve. She seemed to have the wisdom of her ancestors, many of whom were destroyed by the lack of understanding of humans.

Lesson #11: Sooner or later, we each have to make a conscious decision of whether or not we will live up to our potential.

Eagles are amazing teachers, but just as they cannot ensure each of their eaglets will be successful, we cannot ensure that the people we want to help develop will make it to where they want to go. Some of us even have fears that prevent us from developing ourselves. Ultimately, eaglets of any variety are accountable to live up to their potential by continuing to make focused decisions and dedicating resources toward the direction of that potential. After Maggie was blown out of the nest, for a time, she was traumatized. For the first few days after she returned home she hunkered low in the nest. When her parents brought her food and tried to encourage her to fly, she cried – she needed to grieve and heal.

At that time Maggie was afraid and, clearly, not the slight bit interested in living up to her potential. But like her parents the season before, her instincts were strong. She began to realize she was at a critical point in her development. She knew she could fly, but she also knew how hard it was to land. She had to master it. But an eagle's life is not just about learning to fly and land. Even more difficult is learning to hunt and fish, all part of soaring to one's potential.

At first Maggie sat on a perch near the nest and cried – for about an hour -- waiting for mom and dad to remedy the situation. Then she began to venture off in search of fish, but she was still quite clumsy. After a short time, she learned that she could catch something... maybe it was not quite dead when she got it to the nest so she sat on it (no violence, just an eagle-oops!). But after her prey was dead she got up, sat on the side of the nest, and had her fish dinner. As the locals observed these sorts of rituals, they began to expect she (and her family) would migrate at any time.

Sometimes the locals would watch poor Maggie struggle. But the main point of this lesson is...if the eagle's mom and dad had just gone to her and fed her because they could not stand to see her sad and crying... she would never have learned to soar! She would just be a big eagle...in a little nest, someone who had never reached her potential. So, when one thinks of how tough it can be to soar to one's potential, it is also important to consider how many people never do – for whatever reasons. It is a way to reframe a situation so that one can understand how blessed one truly is!

Lesson #12: Remain aware and consider the opportunities.

It was Saturday, May 26, 2012 and the Teacher wrote in her journal.

> This morning we rode to the back of the preserve first, stopping to see if Maggie was in her nest. She was not; instead she was atop a perch about 20 feet southwest of her nest. We were earlier (about 8:30am) than we have been in recent weeks and it looked as if we arrived right after Maggie had awoken. She was not yet very active, but she was out of the nest (we don't know that she slept in it).

The Builder and Teacher decided to ride on, giving Maggie time to awaken and traveling round to the bridge where the scope-observers were usually set up. Sure enough! There was the Painter, near a shaded bench with three other locals one of whom had her rescue puppy with her. The Builder and Teacher joined them, chatting for about an hour during which time several bikers stopped to observe Maggie on her perch.

When Maggie decided it was time to soar, the Builder, the Painter, an artist and the Teacher were all together – they watched her lift high in the air. Up she went, in her corkscrew climbing effect. Quickly, they each scrambled to capture her on film – as they "oooohhhh, ahhhhhh'd" and cheered her on – up into the sky. Suddenly, someone called out, "Her parents are soaring with her!" Sure enough, the two adult eagles were even higher up – and Maggie was climbing toward them. Then she changed course. Independently she flew toward the bay where the locals hoped she would be learning to catch her own lunch. They were all delighted! Each person thought synchronously,

"It doesn't get any better than this! Not only have we seen the whole family flying together this morning, we have seen them when we are all together!"

Each person realized the eagle family would move on soon – and they realized how amazingly blessed they were to have been able to participate in such a miraculous adventure. When the Builder and the Teacher traveled back to the nest area of the Preserve, Maggie was home again, perched high on one of the roosts from which Mom and Dad so diligently observed and nurtured her as she has matured over the past few months. Maggie was alone there, as if she was taking time to let the locals down easily. Soon the Builder and the Teacher would literally be among the small community of empty nesters looking forward to the eagles' migratory return.

It was June 2, 2012. The Teacher wrote in her journal, "The family flew together again today!"

The locals all knew that the birds were preparing to go. In recent weeks, the older eaglets, who were now two-year-old adolescents, had returned to the nest area to determine how Mom, Dad and Maggie were going to proceed. One more lesson had been imparted to the locals. Eagles and people must be aware of change and the environment. We must consider what resources are available, how to remain stewards of our resources, and how to continue developing resources – to remain aware of the opportunities that emerge before us and to nurture the relationships that strengthen us. Those who want each of us to develop our potential know the true meaning of love. They know the true value of relationships – between the eagles, between locals and the Preserve, between the locals as a group, and in many other aspects of the locals' lives.

June 2, 2012, the Teacher sent out an email to the eagle-watcher-locals of the Preserve,

"We are having an 'eagle stories party' on Friday evening at the Preserve to celebrate how wonderful getting to know them (and each other) has been. We hope you can make it. It would not be the same without your presence."

# Chapter 11 – Learning is a Never Ending Process

Maggie on her first solo flight, high above the Teacher for the
first time in May 2012

By Friday, the night of the eagle celebration, the locals realized they had all been witnesses to a magnificent family story. They had observed two eagles overcome huge obstacles, and build a home for their family - over and over again. They had watched the pair of birds prepare to raise, lift up, mentor, and develop the next generation so that it would soar even higher than the parents who had so exquisitely taught them how. The locals realized that the two adult eagles had done such an outstanding job of this process previously that the two adolescent eagles had not wanted to leave their side. In fact, one adolescent eagle was spotted in the nest by the Teacher and the Builder just shortly after the parents and Maggie had gone. The adolescent seemed to signal that its parents and younger sibling had gone traveling for the summer. The young bird seemed to be waiting, looking north, and arranging twigs to prepare the nest for summer. Its actions seemed to say,

"I'll make the nest ready for you." Again, the message was biblical, a visual representation of the 23rd Psalm.

Both the Teacher and the Builder knew that by the time the adult birds returned, the adolescent would be soaring elsewhere, probably in the early stages of seeking a mate of its own. After all, the adolescent birds were almost three now, and by the time their parents returned, they would be between ages three and four, when the birds start looking for the love – and the partner - of their lives. For them, the cycle of developing new eagle families, and mentoring their young would continue on - from generation to generation, as beautifully as it has been passed down through the ages. For humans who are astute enough to notice, the lessons would continue, making us realize how magnificent these role models are for us and others.

Yes, when the eagles finally took off for their summer destination, the people who had observed them at the Preserve gathered as a community. They each brought their best dish, celebrating an early summer Thanksgiving, for that was exactly why they met. Each of the locals began to realize the many ways in which their lives had been touched by the lessons they had learned from the eagles. Each local began to consider some of the things they had learned, and how their life would never be as it was, since it had been enhanced by the 'presents' from the eagles.

For instance, the Rangers more deeply appreciate their meaningful work than ever before. They have continued to find that as they put forth efforts to care for and honor the Preserve, their gifts, like those of the eagles, have multiplied. And, each of their efforts, the gifts of their labor, has been interpreted differently by locals, according to each person's needs.

The government officials involved in acquisition of the Preserve have continued to view the community, and their roles as stewards, in an increasingly expansive light. They too have gained an important eagle perspective. Each time an opportunity for the community to acquire new Preserves arises, they strive to examine the situation and to act in the interests of the people, the environment, and the marvelous creatures that are indigenous to the area. It appears as if everyone understands that they must treat the gifts with which they have been entrusted with reverence, respect and honor. These are gifts that cannot be replaced - and Humphrey's Preserve continues to thrive!

The Humphrey family has continued to be appreciated by everyone who visits the Preserve – if only indirectly. Their choice to behave as responsible citizens has made a remarkable difference in the lives of many. People from all over the world visit the Preserve, and everyone who visits the place is learning to cherish it. Through that they may also learn ways to better cherish the places near where they live. After all, restoration is an ongoing and rewarding process that many humans are participating in all around the world. Humphrey's Preserve has become a shining example of how and why people do that – and the eagles play an ongoing role in demonstrating the rewards and importance of such efforts.

The Painter still visits the Preserve regularly, and he volunteers on a continuing basis. He is perceived by many to be one of the resident eagle experts. He has made many new friends, taught many nascent eagle watchers, and told many a story about Maggie and her parents. He also took a remarkable risk as a result of participating in his many newfound relationships. The Painter found himself involved in a fledgling dating relationship with a wonderful woman who also frequents the Preserve. She too is an eagle watcher. And, although the relationship may or may not work out for both of them, they both were once terribly lonely, like eagles whose lifelong mates had moved on. Now they are soaring again! The gift the Painter was given by the eagles was a fresh new perspective on life and a renewed trust in relationships. He is learning to trust and to share that perspective with others.

Among the Painter's new relationships is an ongoing friendship with the Builder. Now, the Builder has learned quite a few lessons from the eagles himself. He learned how much he enjoyed filming the birds and other wildlife of the area. By the time the birds migrated, he had hours and hours of video, which he is now making into a documentary – as the beautiful pictures he took are meant to be shared with others. He also realized he has the potential to be an important local historian and naturalist. You may remember that he grew up near the Preserve and witnessed many phases of its development. In fact, his help with writing this story was a critical element. The story could not have been written without his help. He is also the photographer who took most of the photos that have been used to tell this story. Now he is developing his gifts, as well as other photography, at the Preserve and beyond. In fact, (true story!), the Builder not only took several of the photographs that have been used for this book, he also helped to write and edit many of the lessons gained from the eagles. He now accepts the unique perspective the eagles afforded him. He is also increasingly grateful for the place where he grew up, as well as what its unique beauty means to others, birds, humans and other critters alike.

The Builder and the Teacher learned some lessons as a team as well. They have gained a deeper appreciation of their relationship as partners in all aspects of their lives. Like the eagles, they have continued to improve and appreciate their humble, yet strong, nest. They have begun to see their roles as mentors in a more reverent light as well. You see, the Builder and the Teacher, like the eagles, are blessed with multiple of generations of young eagles in their lives, both as family members and as community. And, like the eagles, the Builder and the Teacher, are gaining a deeper relationship as lifelong partners – the loves of each other's lives. Just like the birds, they have weathered storms and had to make difficult decisions. Just like the eagles, and by the eagles, they are reminded "[that] those who hope in the Lord will renew their strength. They will soar on wings like eagles; they will run and not grow weary. They will walk and not grow faint" (Isaiah 40:31, NIV)

As a result of the many lessons the Teacher learned from the eagles, she decided to let go of old and useless relationships that were harming her, her family and other people that she loves. The eagles would want it that way. It is important to let go of that which keeps us from living up to our potential. After all, the eagles had been through, they never forgot how to soar. And, each behavior that they modeled taught the Teacher that she still knew how to soar too. She moved on to teach people in places and situations where her skills and her talents are appreciated. Opportunities of which she became aware were greater than she had previously imagined. They can be when one refocuses according to one's true identity. Yes, the Teacher moved on to work that better fit her talents and identity. And the first of that was that she decided to write the story of the eagle family, realizing that it needed to be shared with a wider audience. It needed to be shared with YOU! And who knows? Perhaps the eagle story is the most important 'course' the Teacher has taught – so far. The presents of the eagles have always been meant to be shared. This story is from the Teacher's perspective.

# Chapter 12 – Lessons from the Eagles Revisited

Maggie in the nest about two weeks before the family
migrated for summer

The parenting model presented and the twelve other lessons introduced in this book are but a few of the 'presents' the locals received from the eagles at the Preserve. The presents are also shared as stories told from the perspective of the Teacher. At times, she shared them with the Builder and with other eagle observers, some of whom agreed and some of whom would tell the stories differently. Life is like that. We each interpret its lessons and events in our own way, through our own filters, with our own intentions and considering our individual motivations.

As time has gone by, each local has continued to realize that many more eagle lessons were imparted. Sometimes reflection, time and experience must be added to extract the full benefit of life's teachable moments. And sometimes it takes a while to recognize how valuable teachable moments, and life's lessons truly are. The Teacher and the Builder still enjoy many conversations about what a remarkable gift the time and experience with the eagle family truly was. It seemed like a critical mass of students were ready for an important learning experience. And, a Buddhist proverb reminds us that when the student is ready, the master will appear (Buddhist Maxims and Proverbs). This was the case for each of the locals, as well as for the group. It might also explain how each of their learning experiences was uniquely tailored to fit the needs of the student. For the Teacher, it was nothing less than divine inspiration.

Now that summer has ended, and activity at the Preserve is abundant, the two adult eagles have been noticed visiting their nest to make minor repairs and alterations. The osprey that spent much of the summer there has been relegated to a nearby perch where he can look, but not touch, their domain. The eagles have been seen individually and together, perched high in the pines that overlook the panoramic view of the Preserve. They remain the symbols of freedom, strength, and dignity that humans have revered for many hundreds of years.

Some of the locals even say they have seen the young eaglet, but truth be told, no one would know exactly what she would look like by this time. For sure, the physical changes that she has experienced are indefinable by the locals, but some of the locals cannot help but wonder. Would she remember us? Does she know we would love to see her? They can only wait, speculate, and consider the stories she'd tell about soaring to her potential. Many of them are telling stories too – as they soar to their own potential. It is a matter of trust; it is also a matter of faith that all will turn out right.

For example, as Maggie gained self-confidence through the increased trust she learned about from the mentoring she received from her parents, she likely came to understand the rationale behind their fearless parenting. Or is she still learning this? Author Joe Cervasio (2008), suggests that trust-building such as exhibited in eagle parenting is attributable to competence, commonality, intention, and empathy. He compares the relationship to the love Christian Believers experience from and for the heavenly Father, Abba, above.

Likely, the eaglet will not forget the following twelve lessons that her parents imparted to their daughter:

Lesson #1: Always remember, if you were intended to be an eagle that is what you are! Why would you want to try to be anything else? One thing is sure. The eaglet has not forgotten who or whose she is. Once this lesson is learned, one knows exactly who to fly with!

Lesson #2: No matter how many others believe in you, you cannot fly until you believe that you can. Once Maggie got this down, she could soar. Without this lesson, she never would have made it out of the nest!

Lesson #3: Even if you fall out of the nest, don't panic. Remember you know how to survive! When life presented difficult situations, Maggie looked around for her mentors, but she also looked to herself. They reminded her, and she learned to trust their reinforcement. She knew how to survive! She also had phenomenal role models demonstrating exactly what she needed to do.

Lesson #4: No matter what a coyote may tell you, the coyote is not your friend. When Maggie needed help, many voices brought ideas to her 'rescue'. She learned to discern between friend and foe. She learned to consider the speaker's motivation. This helped her to recognize who was her friend or foe.

Lesson #5: Remember to be grateful to your true supporters. You could not have accomplished your goals without them. Just as Maggie learned to discern foe from friend, rescuer from coyote, she also learned the value of expressing her gratitude. Everyone knew when Maggie made it back to her nest! And everyone knew that she was exceedingly grateful for their support!

Lesson #6: Never stop learning. There is always more to know and the environment is constantly changing. Once Maggie got a taste of her potential, she wanted to soar! She needed to continue to develop it. Her parents were supportive. They too knew that learning is a lifelong process. Even when one has mastered a skill, the environment keeps on changing. Survival is contingent on continuing to learn.

Lesson #7: Keep the faith. You didn't make it this far to not continue to succeed. Life is tough! Certainly, Maggie learned that early on. She saw examples of what being faithful meant in front of her in the form of her parents and others. Each success increased her faith, and each success no doubt was stored as a sacred memory that reminded her she could succeed in difficult times. That is the attitude of an eagle!

Lesson #8: Setbacks are just that. They might set you back, but then you carry on. Remember, you are an eagle. If necessary, refer to Lesson #1. Maggie learned early on that it is not how many times one gets knocked down, but how many times one gets back up that matters. She not only got back up, she also learned to soar!

Lesson #9: Timing is important in life. Never fly in such a way that the wind will be against you if you can use it to your advantage; in the spirit of the famous old Irish prayer, 'May the wind always be at your back'. Maggie learned to use her resources wisely. She learned to waste nothing – and because of that she became a master at harnessing the wind, the essential power that would enable her to take care of all the assignments in her life.

Lesson #10: Never, ever take watching eagles or other marvels of Nature for granted. Live within your means with a deep appreciation of everything that contributes to the quality of your life. You may find that you have more than you think you had. Although we cannot actually see inside of her thoughts, Maggie's actions made it clear that once she learned to fly, hunt and fish, she did not spend much time worrying about what she lacked – she spent time celebrating the wonder of all that she had been gifted with. She focused on what she <u>could do</u> rather than what she could not. This was a key factor in achieving success and soaring to her potential.

Lesson #11: Sooner or later, we each have to make a conscious decision of whether or not we will live up to our potential. If Maggie had not decided to try, her parents would have ultimately had to leave her in the nest to discover how to fend on her own. Sooner or later, everyone makes a conscious decision (and lots of little ones!) toward achieving one's potential or, at best, sitting in an uncomfortable nest.

Lesson #12: Remain aware and consider the opportunities. When Maggie was afraid, she could not envision any opportunities. As she grew strong, confident and healthy, she began to see them all around her. Her demeanor changed. She no longer sat in the nest and whined. She stood tall, watchful of the many adventures that no doubt lay ahead.

Like Maggie, the locals will long remember the 'presents' of the eagles. And whether they walk, bicycle, roller skate, or travel in the Ranger rover, they will remain aware and consider the opportunities to learn lessons from the eagles, each other, and the other inhabitants of Humphrey's Preserve. You see, the most amazing thing happened to each of the locals as they observed the eagles. They each gained a new perspective, not only on the birds, but on their community and on themselves as well.

Eagles are known for their penetrating eyes and amazing sense of vision. They have eyesight that enables them to navigate by seeing long distances, so they know what is ahead of them. From promontories, such as the eagles' nest, the family of birds could see a bigger picture than most of the other raptors. As they soar, sometimes as high as 10,000 feet in the sky, their vision becomes ever more expansive. It includes places, objects, and creatures that none of the other raptors can consider from a similar perspective. The eagles' vision enables them to see each of their actions in a broader context, in a way that minimizes the trials of tribulations of daily living and maximizes the importance of their behaviors with regard to history and future generations. Perhaps this is one of the reasons that they have been revered across culture and throughout time.

Like the eagles, the locals began to see themselves more clearly as role models for the 'eaglets' of all ages in their own circles of influence. Each person was dared to consider his or her motives on an ongoing basis. Each local was reminded that we all make regular choices that define the quality of our own lives, as well as our legacy to future generations and our community. The eagles have clearly given magnificent presents to the locals – and we hope that some of those presents have now been passed on to you!

# Chapter 13 – 12 Lessons (the short version)

Lesson #1: Always remember, if you were intended to be an eagle that is what you are! Why would you want to try to be anything else?

Lesson #2: No matter how many others believe in you, you cannot fly until you believe that you can.

Lesson #3: Even if you fall out of the nest, don't panic. Remember you know how to survive!

Lesson #4: No matter what a coyote may tell you, the coyote is not your friend.

Lesson #5: Remember to be grateful to your true supporters. You could not have accomplished your goals without them.

Lesson #6: Never stop learning. There is always more to know and the environment is constantly changing.

Lesson #7: Keep the faith. You didn't make it this far to not continue to succeed.

Lesson #8: Setbacks are just that. They might set you back, but then you carry on. Remember, you are an eagle. If necessary, refer to Lesson #1.

Lesson #9: Timing is important in life. Never fly in such a way that the wind will be against you if you can use it to your advantage; in the spirit of the famous old Irish prayer, 'May the wind always be at your back'.

Lesson #10: Never, ever take watching eagles or other marvels of Nature for granted. Live within your means with a deep appreciation of everything that contributes to the quality of your life. You may find that you have more than you think you had.

Lesson #11: Sooner or later, we each have to make a conscious decision of whether or not we will live up to our potential.

Lesson #12: Remain aware and consider the opportunities. We hope you have enjoyed reading our story about Maggie and her family of eagles. We were inspired to tell it.

In the process of writing the story we learned about many people and organizations across the US, North America and beyond that are working to ensure these beautiful creatures do not disappear from our environment. Some of those organizations are listed in the following chapter. We have provided the organization names and websites as a starting point, just in case you are motivated to contact them. Also, if you would like to contact us, please do so. We can be reached at Lreed7@tampabay.rr.com or 941.705.0042. We look forward to hearing from you.

# Chapter 14 – Eagle Rescue Resources

The following is a list of some of the organizations that have dedicated themselves to care, conservation, rehabilitation and/or restoration of eagles and, in some cases, other endangered wildlife. The list is not exhaustive, but it does give an indicator of the ways people and organizations are attempting to assist these majestic creatures when they are in trouble. As has been said in the previous story, the main threats to eagles are human. This is a well-documented fact throughout the world in the 21st century. If you would like to get involved in assisting any of these organizations, visit their website, contact them, and learn more about what you can do. We hope you find these resources helpful as you learn more about the 'presents' of eagles.

Alaska

Alaska Raptor Center – Sitka, Alaska. http://www.alaskaraptor.org/

California

Wildlife Education and Rehabilitation Center – Morgan Hill, California http://www.werc-ca.org/

Colorado

Birds of Prey Foundation – Broomfield, Colorado http://birds-of-prey.org/

The Nature and Raptor Center of Pueblo, Inc. – Pueblo, Colorado. http://www.natureandraptor.org/

Rocky Mountain Raptor Center – Fort Collins, Colorado http://www.rmrp.org/.

## Connecticut

Sharon Audubon Center – Sharon, Connecticut.
http://www.audubon.org/local/sanctuary/sharon

## Delaware

Tri-State Bird Rescue and Research – Newark,
Delaware http://www.tristatebird.org/

## Florida

Accipiter Enterprises Educational Birds of Prey –
Live Oak, Florida http://www.birdsofprey.net/

Audubon Center for Birds of Prey – Maitland,
Florida. http://www.audubonofflorida.org/

Avian Reconditioning Center – Apopka, Florida.
http://www.arc4raptors.org/

## Georgia

Chattahoochee Nature Center – Roswell,
Georgia. http://www.chattnaturecenter.org/

## Illinois

Flint Creek Wildlife Center – Barrington, Illinois.
http://www.flintcreekwildlife.org/

Illinois Raptor Center – Decatur, Illinois.
http://illinoisraptorcenter.org/

Stillman Nature Center – Barrington, Illinois.
http://stillmannc.org/

Iowa

Macbride Raptor Project – Macbride Nature and Recreation Center, Iowa.
http://www.macbrideraptorproject.org/

Kansas

Kansas Raptor Center – Great Bend, Kansas.
http://www.kansasraptorcenter.com/

Kentucky

Raptor Rehabilitation Center of Kentucky – Louisville, Kentucky. http://members.aye.net/~raptors/home.htm

Louisiana

Heckhaven Wildlife Rehabilitation Center – Lake Charles, Louisiana. http://www.snowhawk.com/heckhaven

Michigan

Lake Milton Raptor Center – Michigan.
http://www.raptorcenter.org/aboutus.asp

Wildlife Recovery Association – Shepherd, Michigan.
http://www.wildliferecovery.org/

Minnesota

National Eagle Center – Wabasha, Minnesota.
http://www.nationaleaglecenter.org/eagle-center-wabasha-mn-about/

The Raptor Center – St. Paul, Minnesota
http://www.raptor.cvm.umn.edu/

Wildlife Science Center – Forest Lake, Minnesota, http://www.wildlifesciencecenter.org/

Missouri

University of Missouri Raptor Rehabilitation Project – Columbia, Missouri. http://www.raptorrehab.missouri.edu/

World Bird Sanctuary – Valley Park, Missouri. http://www.worldbirdsanctuary.org/

Montana

Montana Raptor Conservation Center – Bozeman, Montana. http://www.montanaraptor.org/

Nebraska

Raptor Recovery Nebraska – Elmwood, Nebraska. http://www.raptorrecoverynebr.org/

New Jersey

Raptor Trust –Millington, New Jersey. http://theraptortrust.org/

New Mexico

Talking Talons Youth Leadership – Tijeras, New Mexico. http://www.talkingtalons.net/home/?page_id=56

New York

Berkshire Bird Paradise Sanctuary – Northern New York. http://www.birdparadise.org/goldeneagle/index.htm

Hawk Creek Wildlife Center, Inc. – East Aurora, New York. http://www.hawkcreek.org/

North Carolina

Carolina Raptor Center – Huntersville, North Carolina.
http://www.carolinaraptorcenter.org/

Ohio

Wildlife Haven – Crestline, Ohio.
http://www.wildlifehaven.org/

Oklahoma

Grey Snow Eagle House – Perkins, Oklahoma.
http://www.iowanation.org/Government/eagleaviary.html

Oklahoma Raptor Center – Broken Arrow, Oklahoma.
http://www.okraptors.org/

Oregon

Blue Mountain Wildlife – Pendleton, Oregon.
http://www.bluemountainwildlife.org/

Cascades Raptor Center – Eugene, Oregon.
http://www.eraptors.org/

International Wildlife Rehabilitation Council – founded in 1972 "by individuals concerned about the care and conservation of native wildlife" in California, now global. Eugene, Oregon. http://theiwrc.org/

Pennsylvania

Pocono Wildlife Rehabilitation and Education Center – Stroudsburg, Pennsylvania. http://www.poconowildlife.org/

South Carolina

The Center for Birds of Prey – Charleston, South Carolina. http://www.thecenterforbirdsofprey.org/.

Tennessee

American Eagle Foundation – Pigeon Forge, Tennessee. http://www.eagles.org/

Virginia

Raptor Conservancy of Virginia –Falls Church, Virginia http://www.raptorsva.org/

Wildlife Center of Virginia –Waynesboro, Virginia. http://wildlifecenter.org/about-center

Washington

Hancock Wildlife Foundation – Blaine, Washington, US and Surrey, British Columbia, Canada http://www.hancockwildlife.org/

Raptor Keeper – Bainbridge Island, Washington. http://raptorkeeper.com/Raptor_Rescue.html

Sardis Raptor Center – Ferndale, Washington. http://www.sardisraptor.org/

West Virginia

West Virginia Raptor Rehabilitation Center – Morgantown, West Virginia. http://www.wvrrc.org/

Wisconsin

The Feather – London, Wisconsin.
http://www.thefeather.org/

Fellow Mortals Wildlife Hospital – Geneva, Wisconsin.
http://www.fellowmortals.org/

Hoo's Woods Raptor Center – Milton, Wisconsin.
http://www.hooswoods.org/.

Pineview Wildlife Rehabilitation Center – Fredonia,
Wisconsin. http://www.pineviewwrc.org/

# References

Arcovio, J. [1993] 2009. The Way of the Eagle. Spirit Led Ministries Publishing.

American Bald Eagle Information General Facts. 2012. http://www.baldeagleinfo.com/eagle/eagle-facts.html . Retrieved 4/27/12 .

Ames, H. 2012. Water Birds in Florida. http://www.ehow.com/info_8102400_water-birds-florida.html . Retrieved 8/27/2012.

Buddhist Maxims and Proverbs. 2012. http://oaks.nvg.org/buddhist-proverbs.html Retrieved 10/24/2012.

Cervasio, J. 2008. Eagle Father's Day Sermon info http://joecervasio.typepad.com/goodnews/2008/06/eagle-parenting.html Retrieved 5/26/2012.

Challenger, R. J. 1996. Eagle's Reflection and other Northwest Coast Stories: learning from Nature and the world around us. Heritage Books.

Cultural Significance of the Bald Eagle. 2012. http://en.wikipedia.org/wiki/Bald_Eagle#Cultural_significance . Retrieved 5/26/12.

Daedelus and Icarus. 2012 http://thanasis.com/icarus.htm. Retrieved 5/27/12.

Florida Coalition for Preservation. 2012. http://preservationfla.org/  . Retrieved 8/23/2012.

Florida Cormorant. 2012. http://web4.audubon.org/bird/BoA/F41_G1c.html  . Retrieved 8/27/12.

Florida Fish and Wildlife Conservation Commission. 2012. Gopher Tortoise. http://myfwc.com/wildlifehabitats/managed/gopher-tortoise/ Retrieved 10/14/2012

Florida Shore and Beach Preservation Association. 2012. http://www.fsbpa.com/about_us.html  . Retrieved 8/23/2012.

Florida's Dept. of Environmental Protection. 2012. Florida's Aquatic Preserves http://www.dep.state.fl.us/coastal/programs/aquatic.htm . Retrieved 8/23/12.

Friends of Florida State Parks. 2012. http://friendsoffloridaparks.org  Retrieved 8/27/2012.

Greenleaf, R. K. [1970] 1990. Servant as Leader. Indianapolis: Greenleaf Center for Servant Leadership.

Guidry, J. 2010. An Eagle Named Freedom: My True Story of a Remarkable Friendship. Harper Collins.

Holy Bible, NIV. 2011. Biblica, Inc.

Littleton, C. S., ed. 2002. Mythology: the Illustrated Anthology of World Myth & Storytelling. San Diego: Thunder Bay Press.

Maslow, D. 2012. Successful Parenting and Baby Eagles – Do You Know the Story? http://ezinearticles.com/?Successful-Parenting-and-Baby-Eagles---Do-You-Know-the-Story?&id=5192944 . Retrieved 5/26/2012.

Murray, A. 2009. Wings Like Eagles. Christian Art Publishers.

National Park Service. 2012. Florida http://www.nps.gov/state/fl/index.htm?program=all . Retrieved 8/23/2012.

Nike. 2012. http://en.wikipedia.org/wiki/Nike_(mythology) . Retrieved 5/27/12.

Perseus. 2012. http://edweb.sdsu.edu/people/bdodge/scaffold/GG/perseus.html   Retrieved 5/27/2012.

Pullam, K. 2012. Parenting Like an Eagle. http://www.sermoncentral.com/print_friendly.asp?ContributorID=&SermonID=103625 . Retrieved 5/26/2012.

RavenWing, J. 2000. A Season of Eagles. iUniverse.com, Inc.

Tennyson, A. L. 1851. The Eagle.

www.ingramcontent.com/pod-product-compliance
Lightning Source LLC
Chambersburg PA
CBHW050549280326
41933CB00011B/1778